9781732066656
I0824922

CHANGE THE WORLD!

CHANGE THE WORLD! A RESEARCH BOOK FOR CHILDREN & ADULTS

by Sibylle Peters

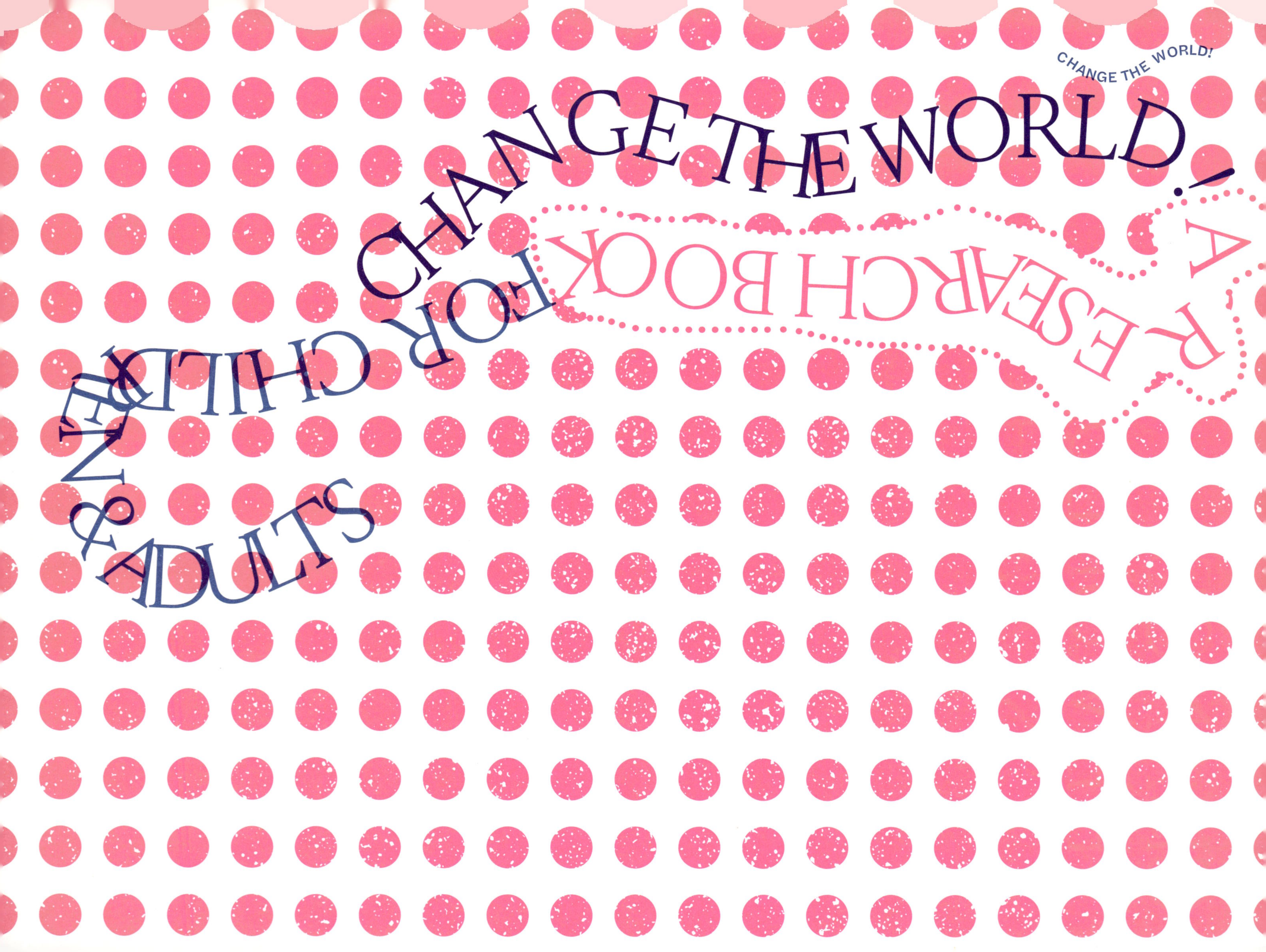
CHANGE THE WORLD!
CHANGE THE WORLD!
A RESEARCH BOOK
FOR CHILDREN & ADULTS

THIS IS A BOOK FOR CHILDREN AND ADULTS, FOR FAMILIES, SCHOOL CLASSES, HOLIDAY CAMPS, AND SO ON.

IT IS BEST FOR CHILDREN AND ADULTS TO READ OUT LOUD AND START RESEARCHING TOGETHER RIGHT AWAY. IT CAN BE READ CHAPTER BY CHAPTER WITH LOTS OF TRYING OUT IN BETWEEN.

Have you ever heard that for small children the world is an enchanted place—a place to meet pirates and travel to space and print your own money? Were you ever told that, when you're eight or ten, you have gotten too old for that and it was all just play, just fantasy—that the world is just the way it is, and you should come to terms with it?

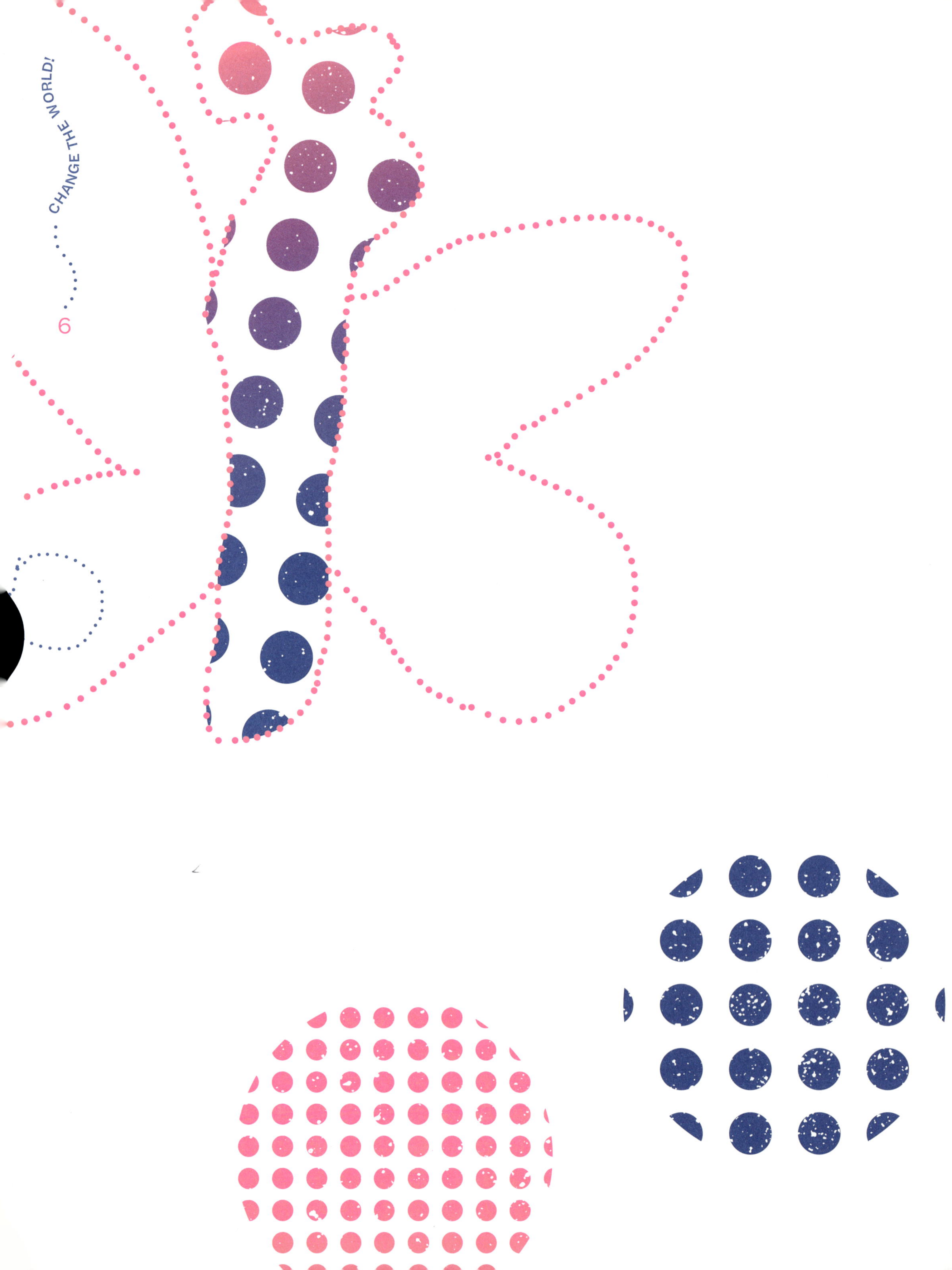

Please, don't believe that. It's nonsense. Really. And we can prove it.

We are from Theatre of Research.[1] Theatre of Research is a place where children and adults do research together. We explore and test new ways of doing things. What we research often has to do with the wishes of the children who take part. And with the fact that we all seem to wish the world to be different than it is. Do you wish that, too?

Since we are a theater, we are particularly interested in how play and reality are intertwined. We'd like to find out how to change reality while playing. Sometimes that works. In any case, at Theatre of Research, we have met pirates and traveled into space and we have printed our own money and much more. We really have. In this book we want to tell you about our research adventures and reveal a few of our research tricks. We hope you will find this useful if you want to do your own research and change reality while playing.

1 Theatre of Research is called FUNDUS THEATER / Forschungstheater in Germany. Theatre of Research was developed within FUNDUS THEATER. FUNDUS THEATER / Forschungstheater is a publicly funded theater venue for young audiences in Hamburg, Germany. Our team consists of Hannah Kowalski, Hanno Krieg, Sibylle Peters, Christopher Weymann, all the people working at FUNDUS THEATER / Forschungstheater, and all the kids, worldwide, who took part in our research.

CHANGE THE WORLD!

TABLE OF CONTENTS

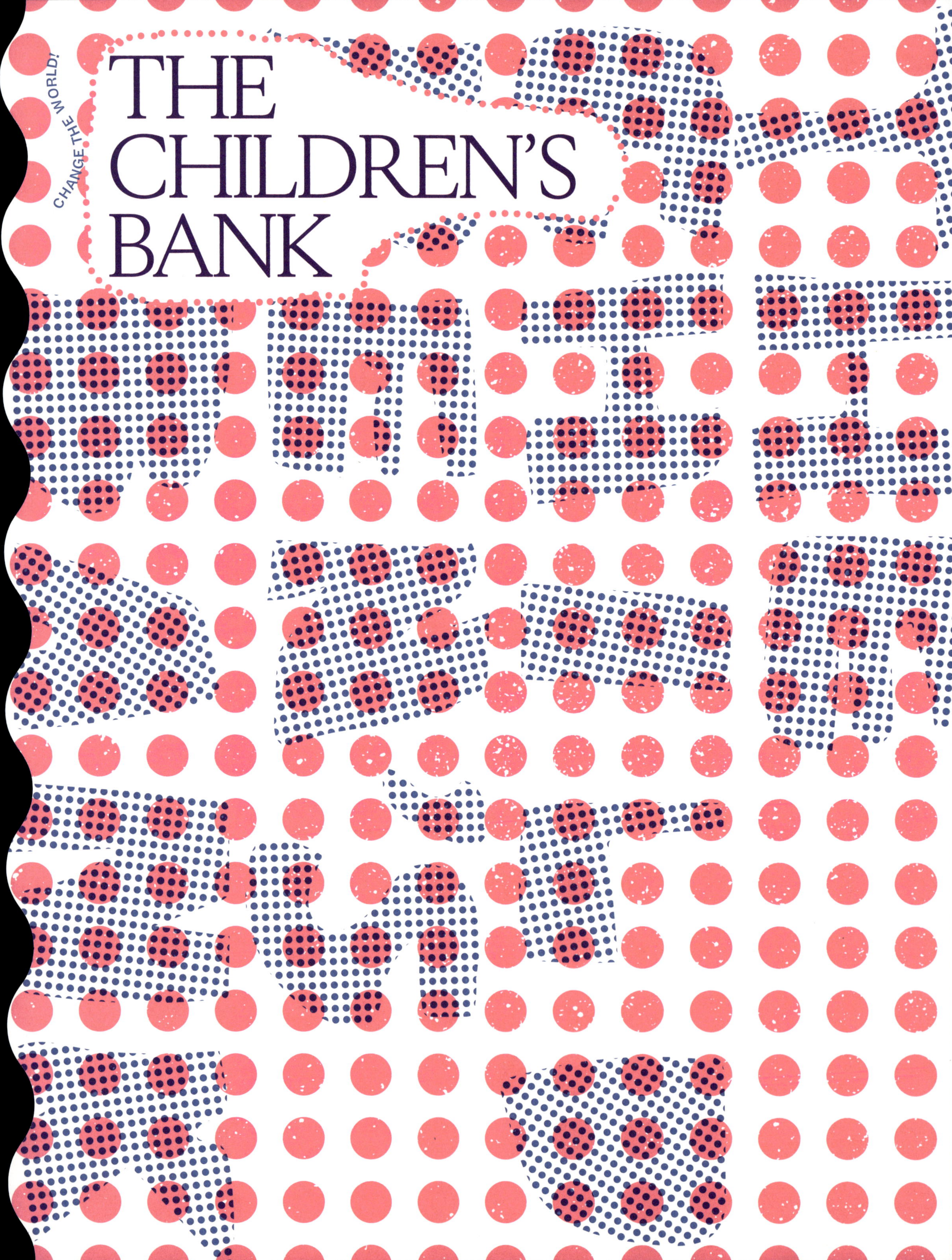
CHANGE THE WORLD!
THE CHILDREN'S BANK

Imagine a fairy appears and grants you three wishes. What are your wishes?

Space for your wishes:

1.

2.

3.

Wishing for a wishing machine or an infinite number of wishes isn't allowed!

In our experience, children are often better at wishing than adults. Why do you think that is?

For example, children at our theater wished:

I want to be friends with animals.

I want to break something.

I want to be rich.

I want to travel to space.

I want to be a pirate.

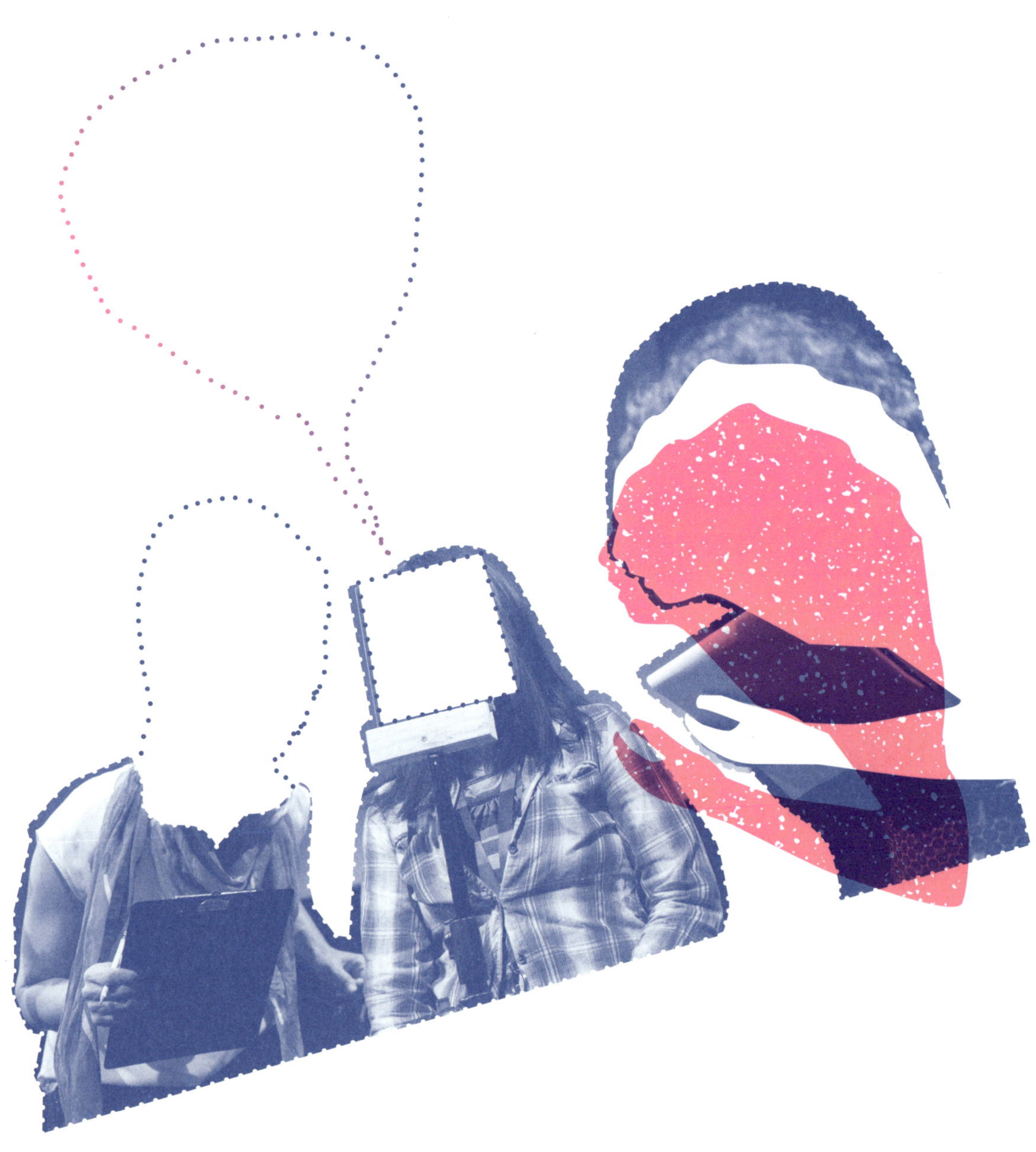

Which of these wishes do you think is the most common?

Exactly. A lot of children wish to be rich. At some point we asked one of them: What does being rich mean to you? *Well, that we can always pay the electricity bill*, said the child. Did you know that children are often much poorer than adults? And being rich is very desirable when you are poor. No question. Unfortunately, we didn't know how to work towards fulfilling this wish. Theaters never have much money either, and besides, you don't

play

with money, right?

Then something amazing happened: The banks went bust.[2] Until then, everyone else was going bankrupt once in a while, but not the banks. But now the time had come: Many banks were somehow broken and you could peek into the bank machine for a moment. Did you know that banks don't just store and transfer other people's money? No, they invent the money themselves. If a bank gives someone a loan, that is, lends them money, they just type the number into the computer and suddenly it IS money. Imagine that.

The moment the banks went bust, everyone suddenly realized that people *do* play with money and that money is very much a game, just a very big one, and if no one played, there would be no

2 This happened worldwide during the financial crisis of 2008.

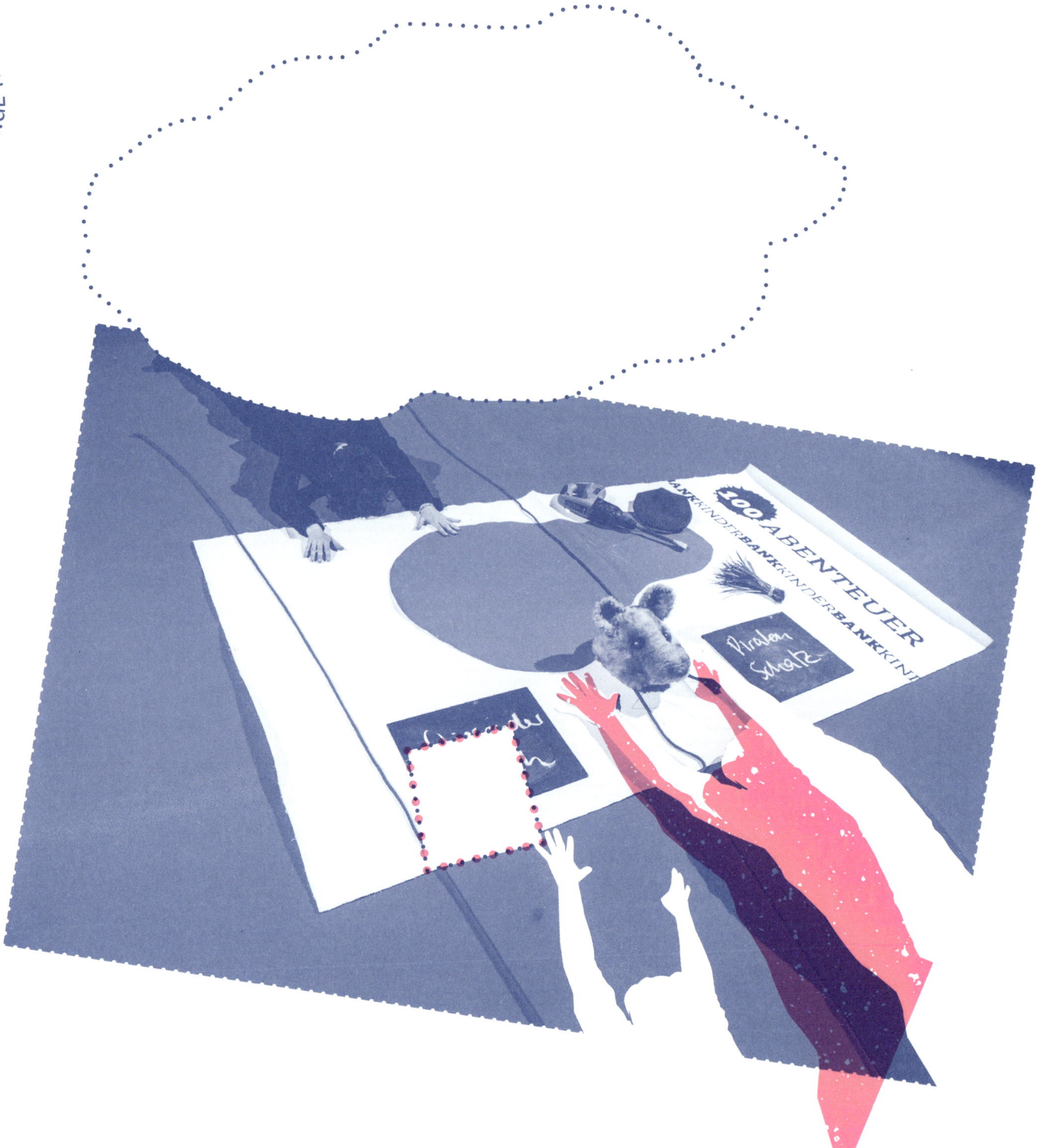

money. When the banks went bust, it wasn't the people running the banks who got into trouble. Instead, a lot of other people didn't have a job or a home anymore. So, everyone realized that

the money game is not fair.

It was clearly time to ask: Can we play the money game differently, can we change the rules? Many people around the world raised this question and some have even tried to change things.

For example, there is Banco Palmas in Brazil. It was started by people in a very poor neighborhood of the city of Fortaleza. Banco Palmas printed its own money for the neighborhood, and the shops and businesses in the district joined in, so that people could actually pay for things with money from Banco Palmas. It made sense to earn the home-made money, and so suddenly lots of new jobs and shops sprung up in the neighborhood. Theatre of Research contacted Banco Palmas and they taught us about the business of alternative banking. Together with children from our district in Hamburg, we founded the Children's Bank[3] and printed our own money. Would you like to try that, too?

3 The Children's Bank of Hamburg was organized by Theatre of Research in 2011 in collaboration with the Black Bank of Oberhausen, a project by the artist group geheimagentur / Secret Agency. It went on until 2017 in different formats, which included a participatory lecture performance and new children's banks opening up in Denmark and Sweden in cooperation with Live Art Denmark.

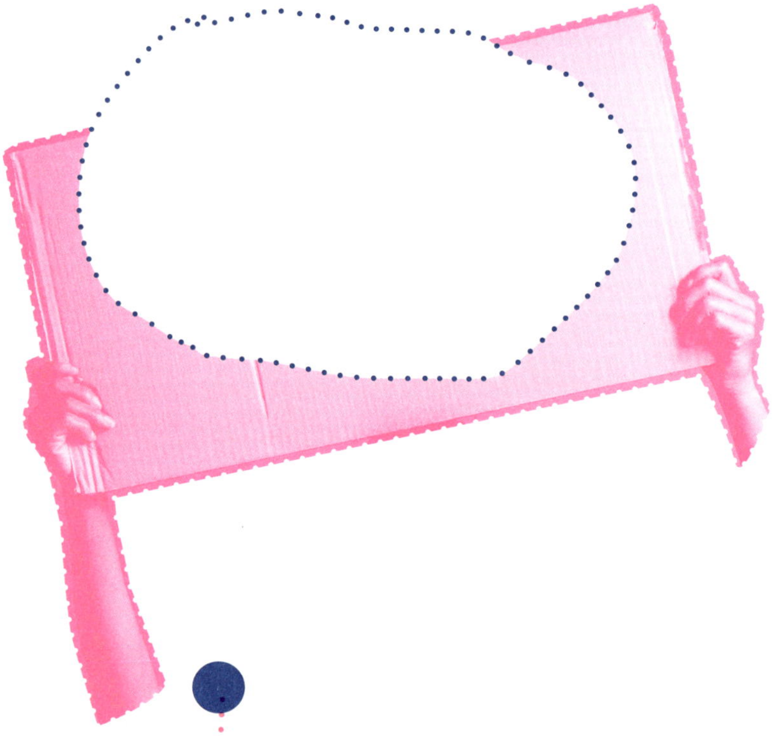

HERE IS A SEVEN-STEP GUIDE TO PRINTING YOUR OWN MONEY:

1. Decide what your money should look like and be called.

In our bank, for example, the children called the money *adventure money* because you could actually have adventures with a bill of one hundred adventures. The kids also decided that

all the bills should be one hundreds.
The bank was meant to make them

rich,

after all.

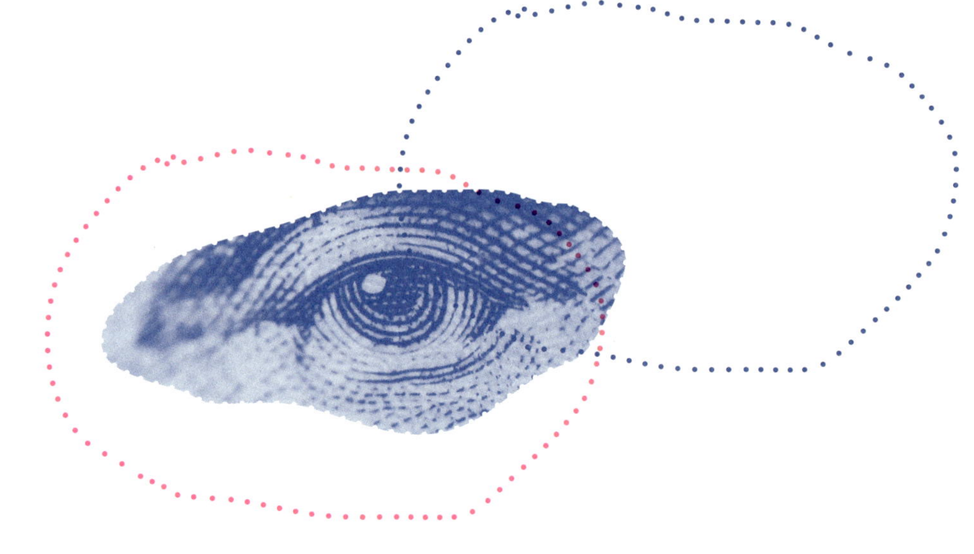

2. Then, find shops who will accept your money. Small, local, corner shops are best suited for this, as you will be able to speak to the boss of the shop directly.

You might wonder: Why would shopkeepers want to participate? The great thing about our adventure money was that only children were allowed to pay with it. So, if the children brought along an adult, and the adult then wanted to buy something, too, the adult would have to pay with dollars, or euros in our case. In our city, small shops often lost customers to the big malls, therefore they were mostly happy to get to know their neighbors and find new customers. Moreover, to participate in the Children's Bank network, the shops would only have to offer one thing in exchange for adventure money, like pencils or soup or grapes. It was also possible that something was offered for adventure money that is otherwise not for sale, such as being allowed to sit in the shop window or get a half-hour table tennis lesson. Of course, not all shopkeepers were interested, some were even a bit rude to us. As you certainly know, kids are often not taken seriously.

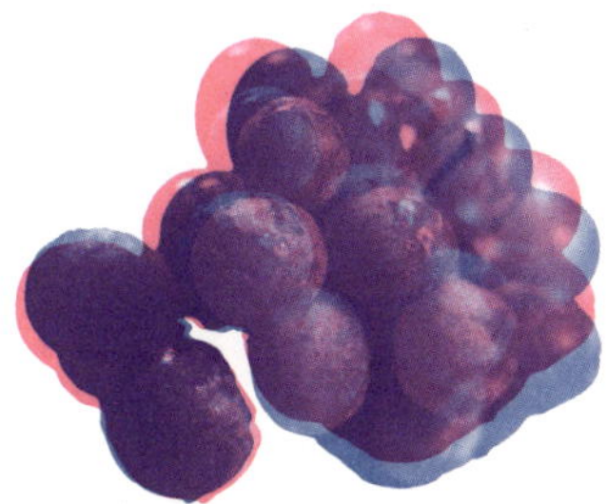

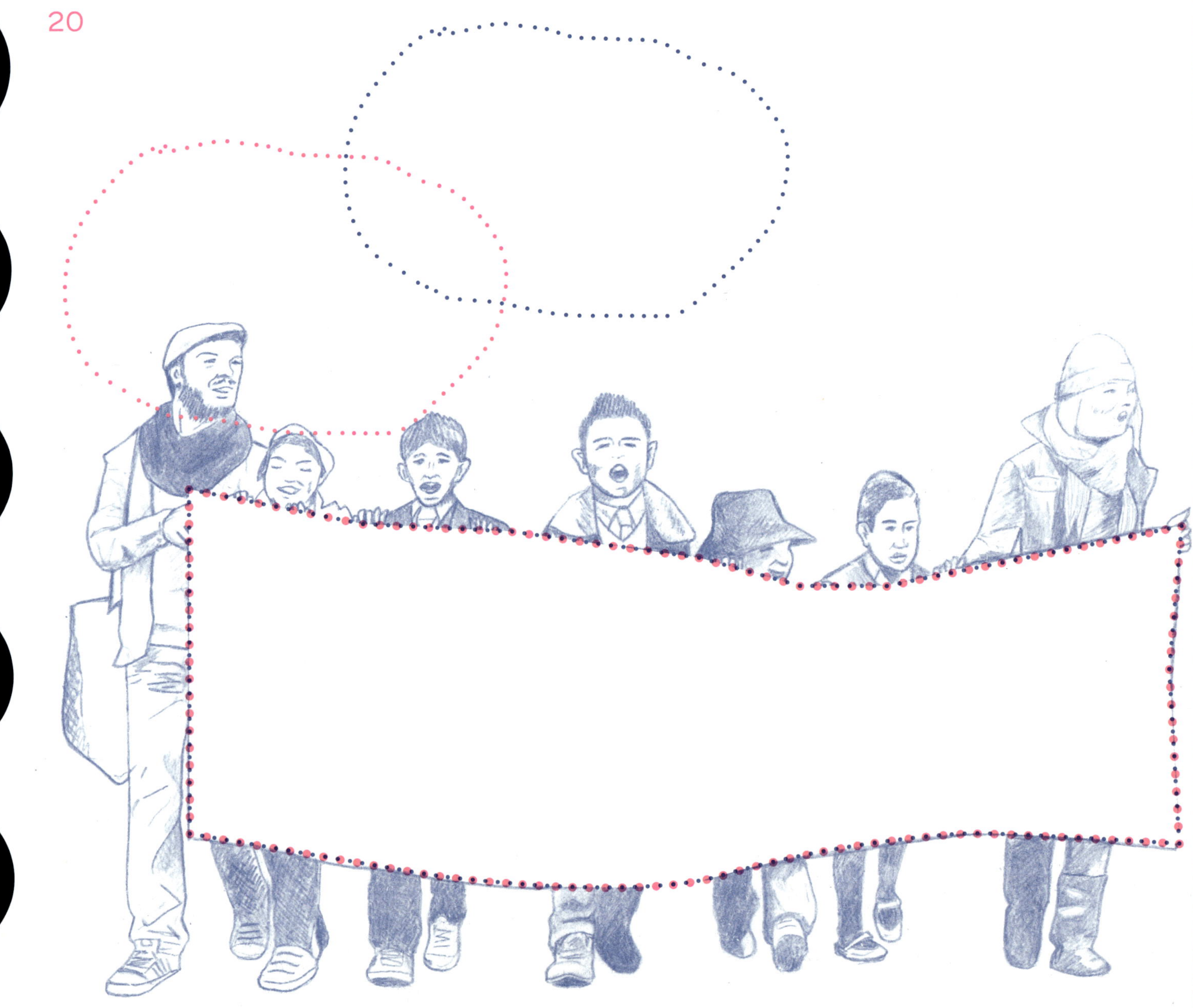

3. When you have convinced at least five shops to join in, you can start printing money. For example, five bills for each child who joins the bank. This way every participating child can shop once in each of the participating shops.

We also created a map of the shops and a Children's Bank sign that shop owners could put in their windows.

4. Now you can go shopping with the homeade money. Mark the moment! Document what you experience. After all, homemade money doesn't happen every day! You might also record interviews or take a few photos as evidence.

The first time we went on a shopping tour with the adventure money, it felt like a party.

We were very excited to try out our money. We split into several groups and met afterwards for a celebratory procession through the streets of our neighborhood.

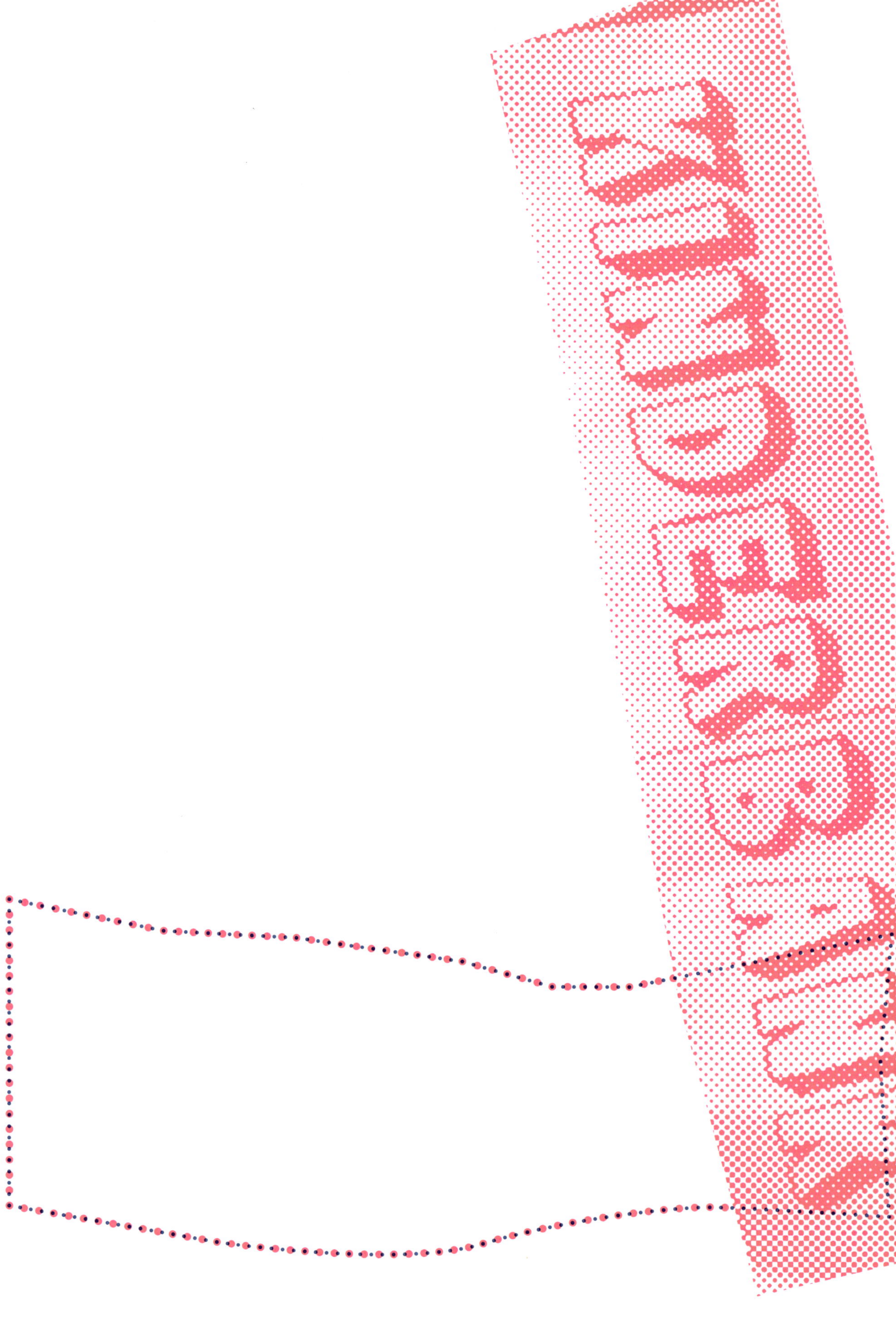

5. When you have spent the first round of money, you should invite all participating children and adults to a Children's Bank meeting. The shop owners too, of course. Here you can report on what you have experienced with the new money.

In our bank, to take part in the bank assembly was special: The participating kids shared their experiences with the adventure money and made everybody feel like part of a community. A community created by money, weird isn't it? In our neighborhood, more than twenty shops got involved. Lots of different people came to the assemblies:

shopkeepers
and
children
and
artists,
experts on poverty
and on
banks,

parents
and
students
and
teachers,
and so on.

Together we learned a lot about money.

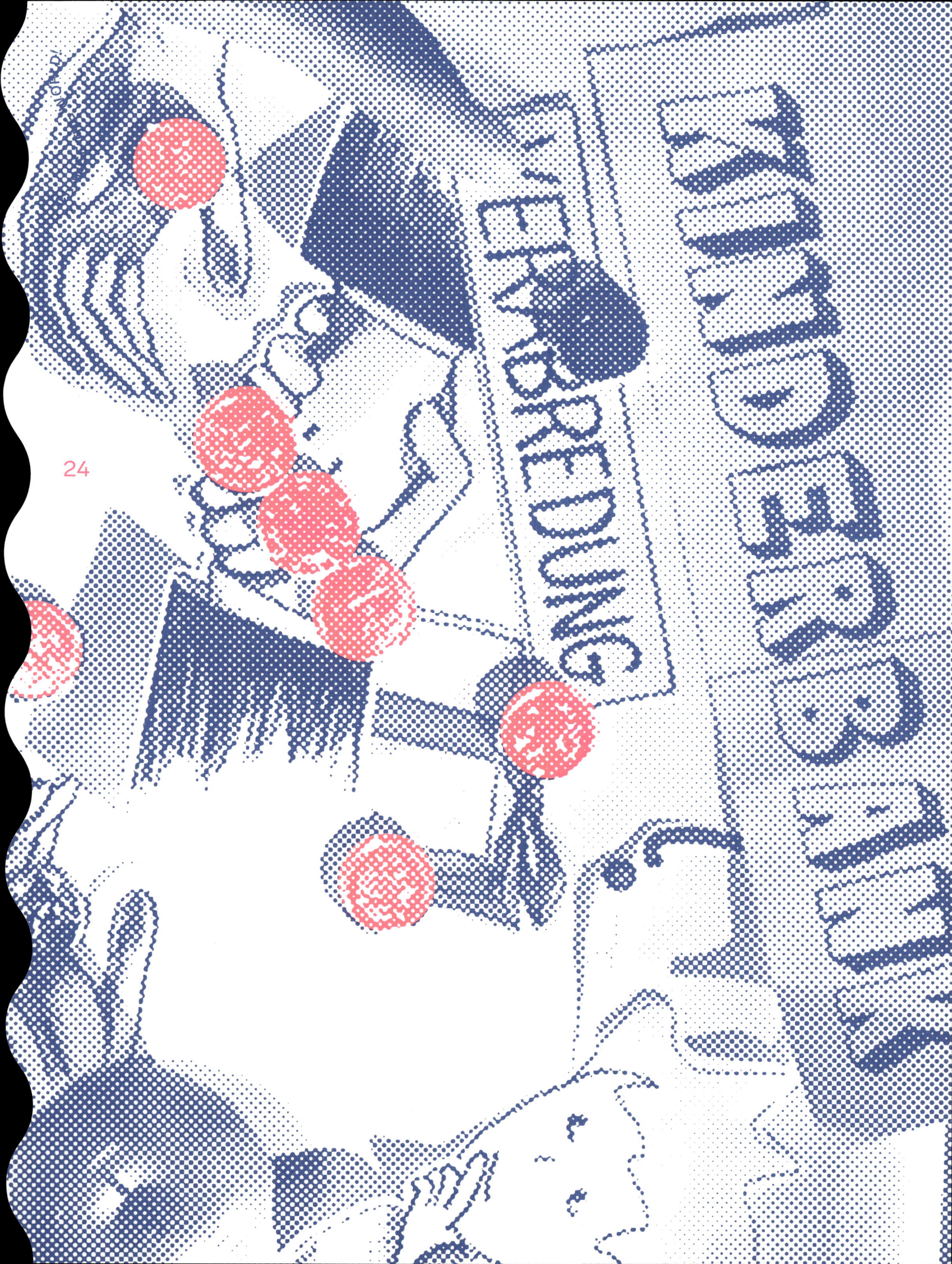
KINDERBAN
ERABREDUNG

6. Then the Children's Bank assembly decides together on how much new money should be printed.

In our bank we learned this: the **more** shops that participate, the **more** money you can print. For a while our bank was growing, because new members also found new shops for the network. We called our bank a gift economy, because our money was not based on work, but on building a community.

7. And so it can go

on

and

on.

More shops and new offers can be added, and more children might want to join and participate. The bank assemblies can also be used to talk about the neighborhood: Does life improve with the new money?

Most people who took part in our bank agreed, that yes, life had improved. But there were also difficulties: Some of the children started trading the adventure money with each other and were confronted with demands like: *If you want to play with us,*

you have to pay for it. The children complained about this at the Children's Bank meeting and made us all think: When does money make sense at all and when does it not?

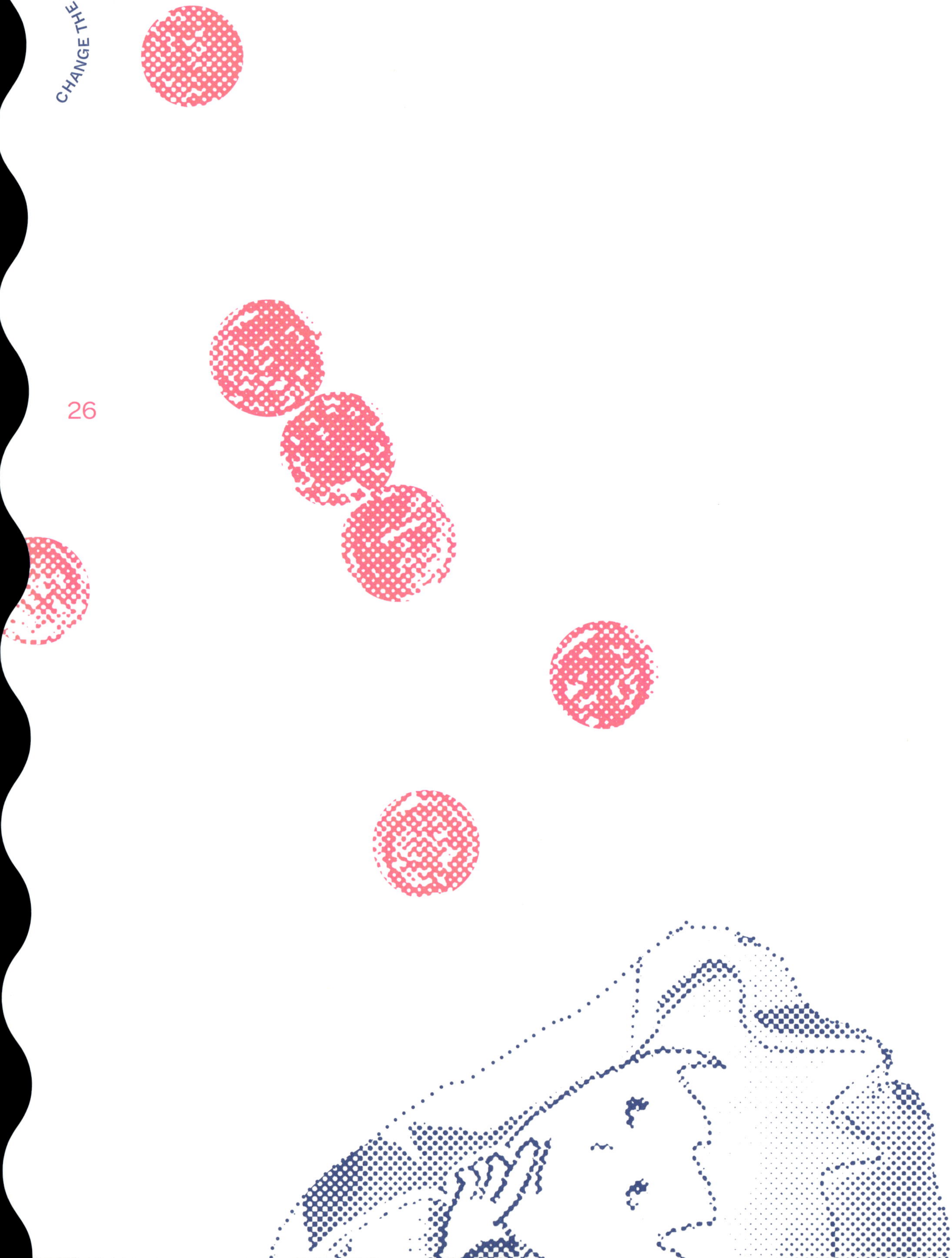

What do you think?

Also, we have to admit one thing: Unfortunately, you couldn't pay the electricity bill with the homeade money. So, we weren't sure whether or not, with the Children's Bank, we had actually fulfilled the wish to become rich. The children were not sure either: You couldn't pay the electricity bill, but at least you could play video games for an hour at the electronics store on the corner with some adventure money if there was no electricity at home. That was something.

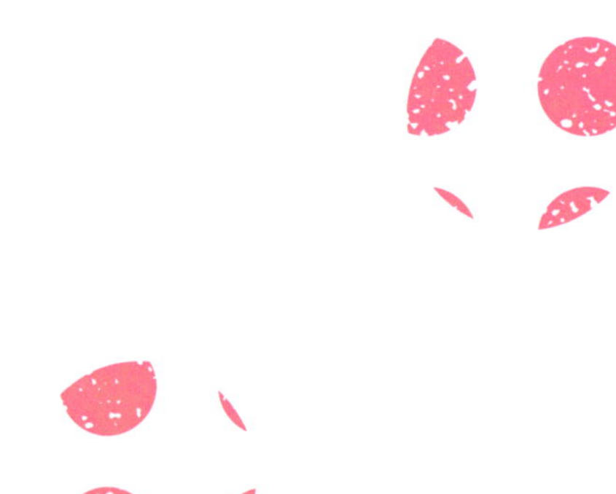

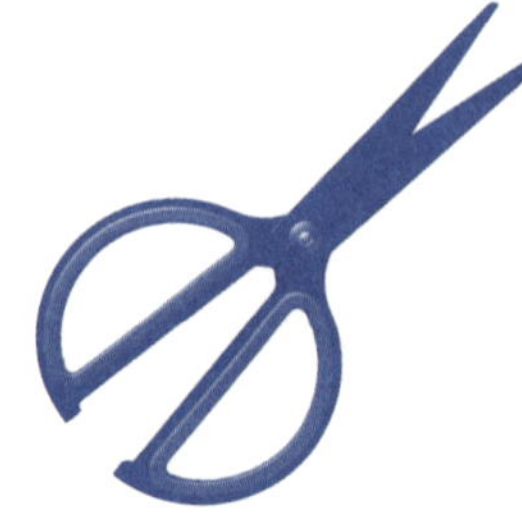

Here you can design your money:

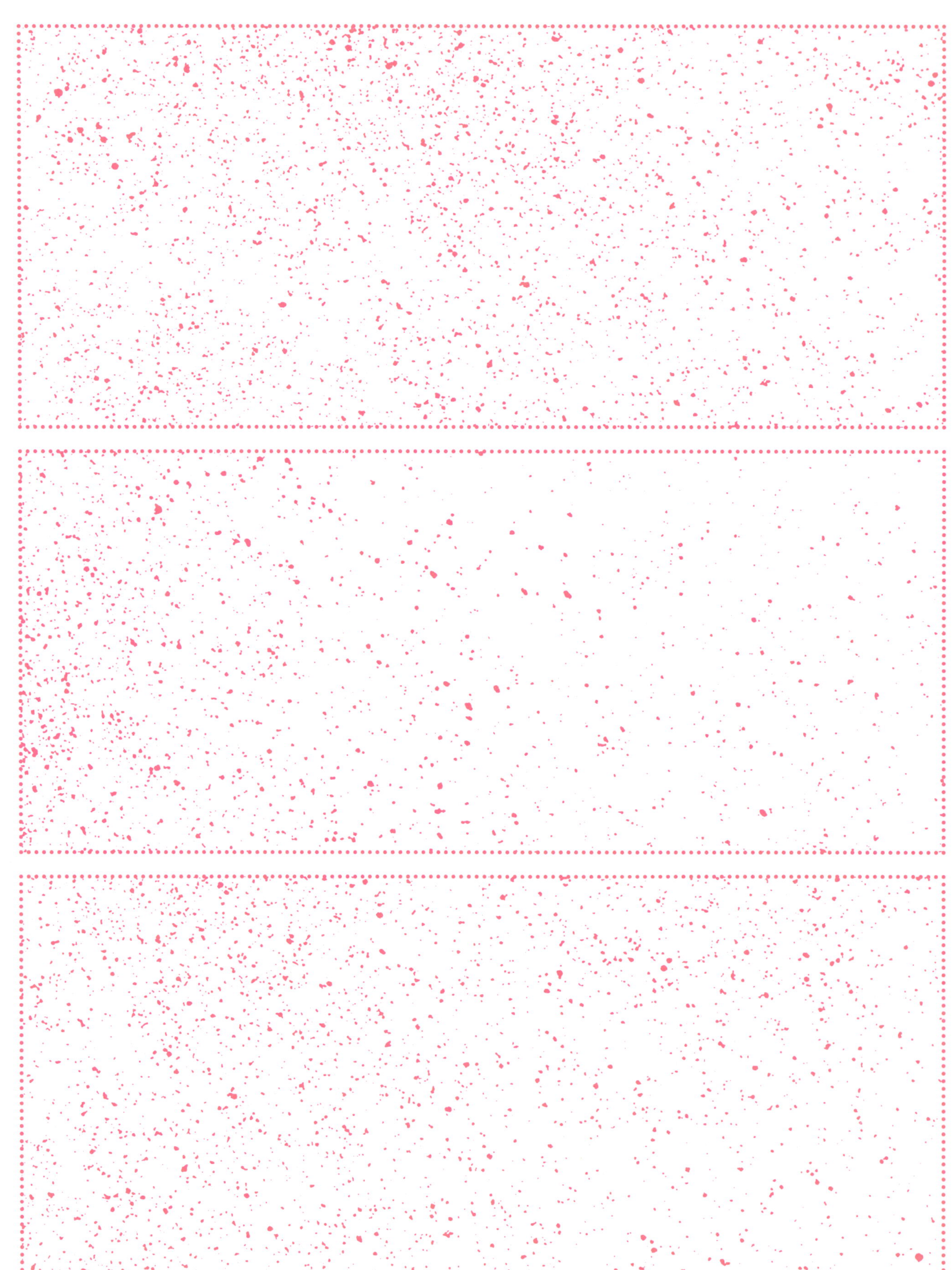

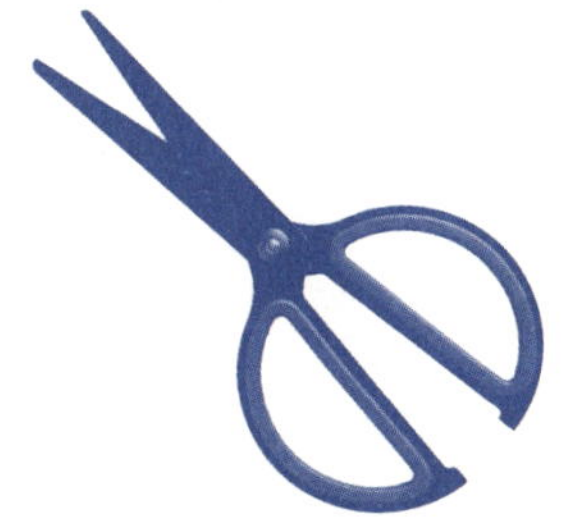

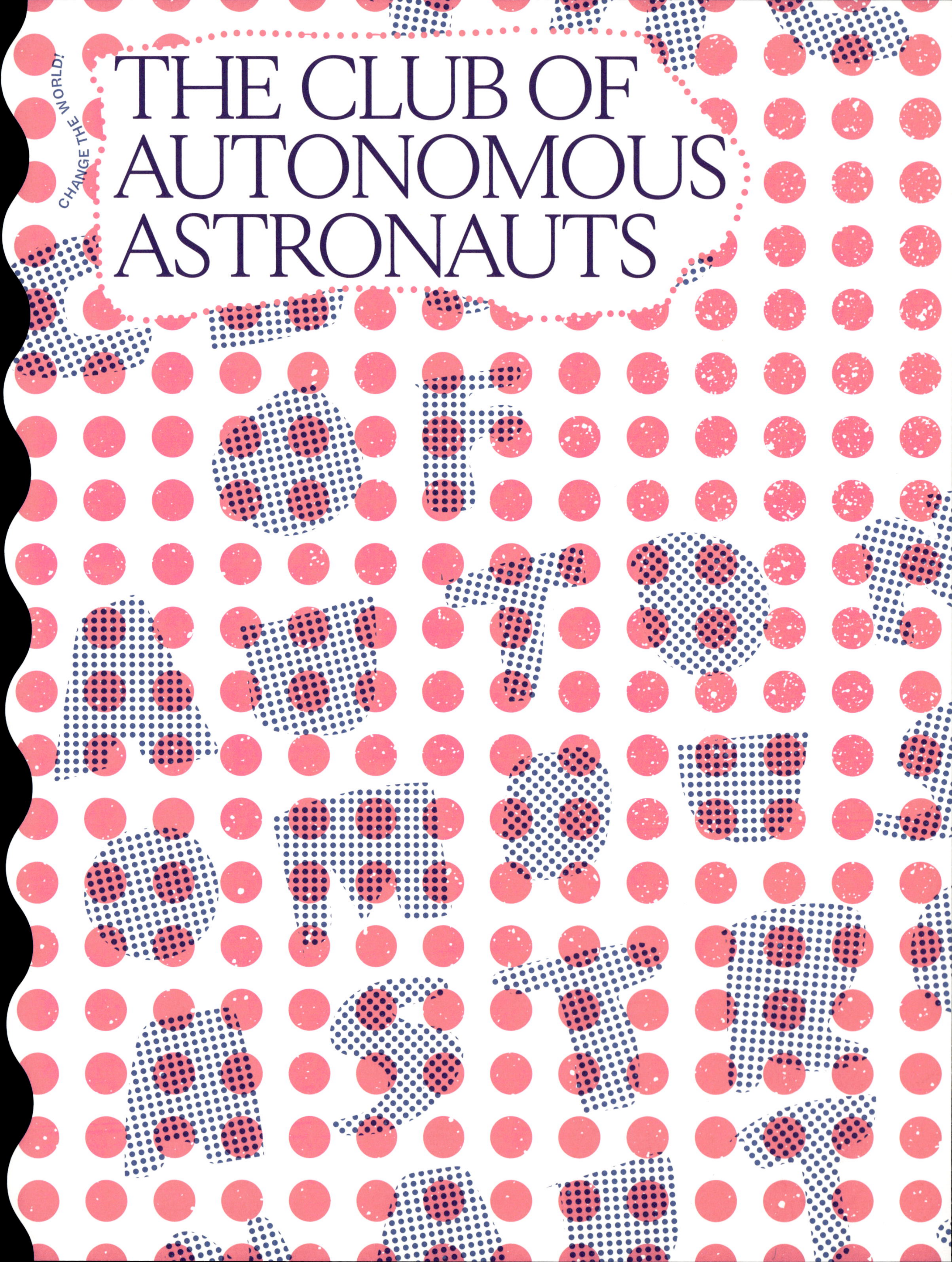
CHANGE THE WORLD!
THE CLUB OF
AUTONOMOUS
ASTRONAUTS

Have you ever wished you were an astronaut? There seem to be two possibilities to fulfill this wish:

If you have money, you can buy lots of stuff: astronaut costumes, movies, games, indoor planetariums, and so on. Then you can play and pretend you're an astronaut.

Or you can try to get really good at mathematics. Because to actually become an astronaut, you first have to study engineering or something and maybe even join the military. And then — after about fifteen years of hard work and a good portion of luck — you have a one in 2,481 chance of being selected for a space shuttle mission. Yeah.

Play or reality. That's the way the world works, isn't it?

What if there was a third option? A third way into space? A path that is both play AND reality? To find this third way, Theatre of Research founded the Club of Autonomous Astronauts.[4] Would you like to become a member?

Design your membership card:

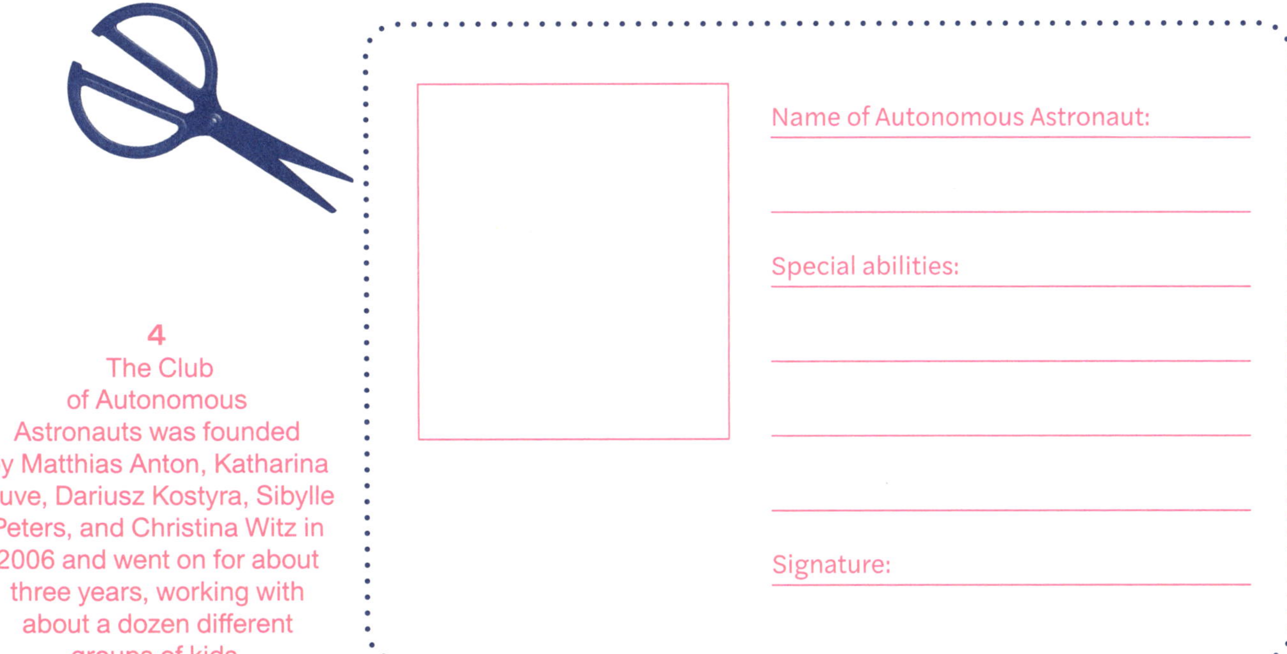

4 The Club of Autonomous Astronauts was founded by Matthias Anton, Katharina Duve, Dariusz Kostyra, Sibylle Peters, and Christina Witz in 2006 and went on for about three years, working with about a dozen different groups of kids.

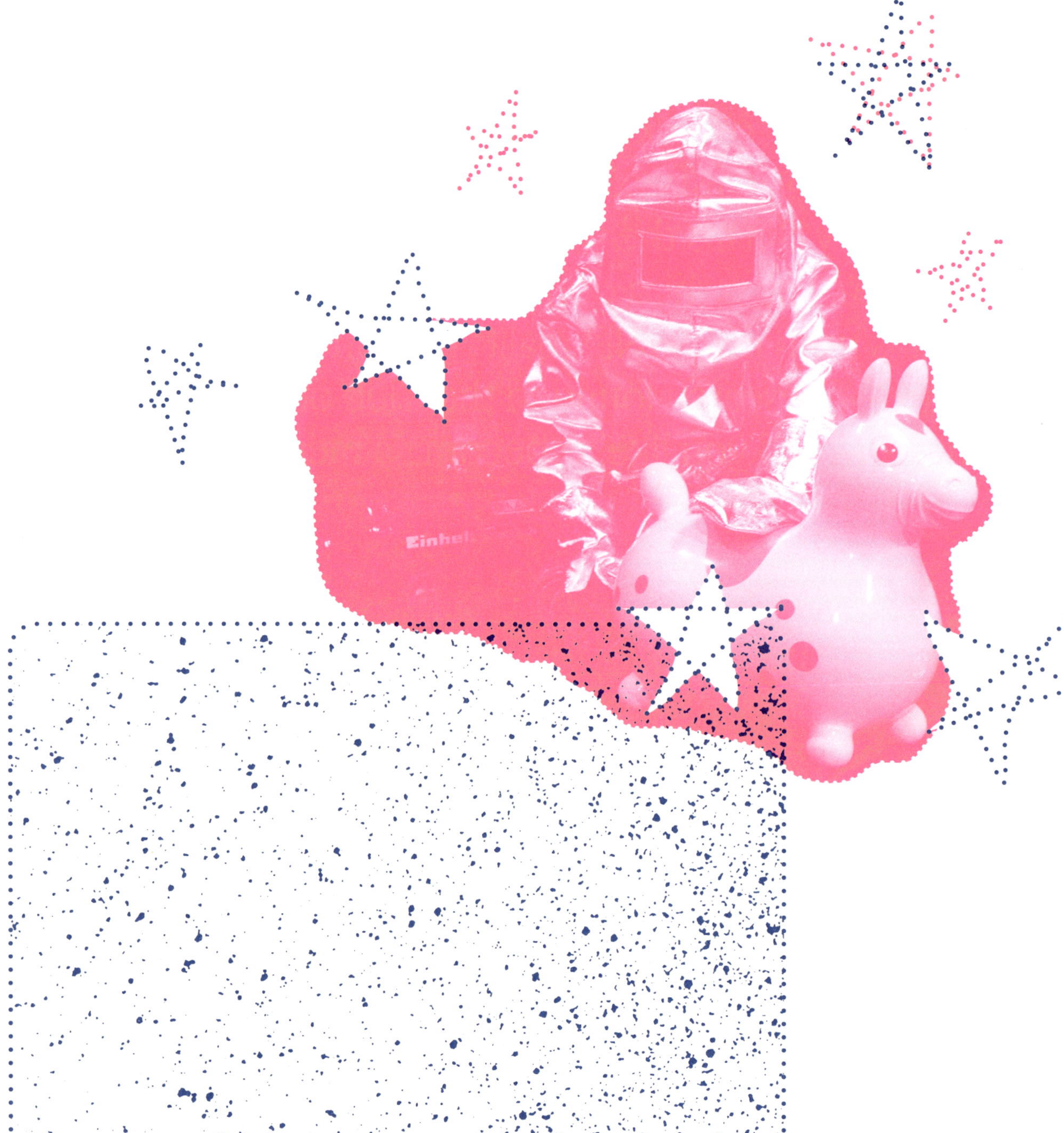

The first people to leave the Earth in rockets said that the best thing about space travel was looking back at our own planet. There they were, in their little tin can in the middle of the ice-cold nothingness of space, and they felt a little bit silly. Because before their eyes floated the most beautiful, most improbable spaceship of all time: the mother ship, blue and white and green, incredibly alive and unique and precious in all that blackness. Suddenly, going into space didn't make much sense anymore. Because there it was, spaceship Earth, flying through the universe at high speed. Everything and everyone on it WAS already in space. They just didn't notice.

That's what the Club of Autonomous Astronauts is all about: we are astronauts on the most beautiful spaceship there is. Most of the time we just don't notice it. We think the Earth is down here and the exciting universe is up there. How can we change that? How can we switch from everyday life to space travel? This is easier said than done. Just to say *hey, we're already in space!* is not enough. When we said that, the kids in the Club of Autonomous Astronaut were sort of disappointed and said: *If we were in space, wouldn't we be able to fly?* That's why we came up with a training course for Earth Astronauts. It's called Flying While Lying. Would you like to try?

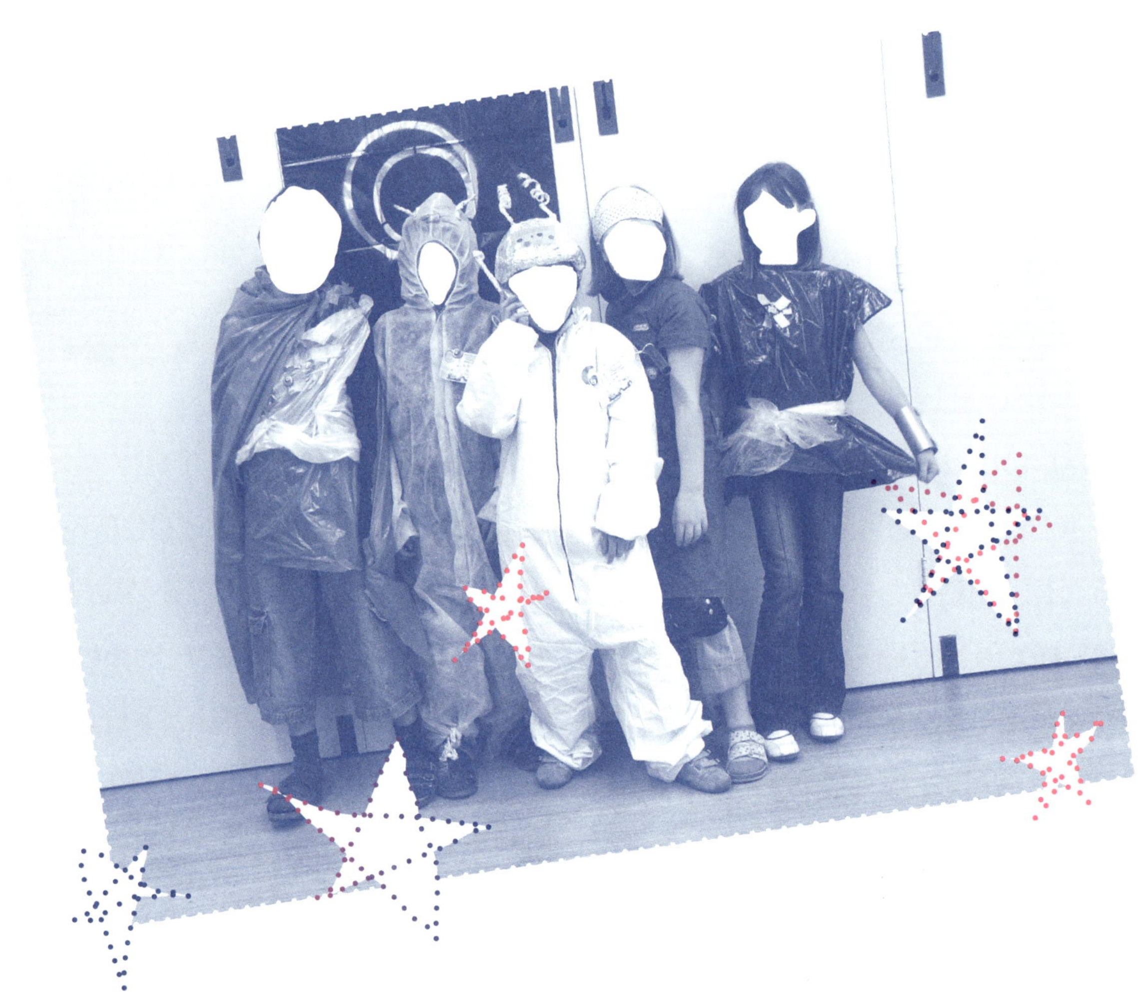

FLYING WHILE LYING TRAINING COURSE

1. For the Earth Astronauts' training you first need a space suit. A huge garbage bag with holes for your head and arms will do, so you can lie down on the ground outside without getting dirty or wet. Of course, you can decorate the garbage bag, for example with silver tape, so that it looks more like a space suit.

2. Now you have to find your seat in the spaceship. Find a place outside where you can lie on your back and look at the sky. What is important, however, is that it is an unusual place where you would not normally lie down. And it should be safe. Like a public space with no cars.

3. Now look at the sky. Do you see the sun or at least know roughly where it is? Do you know that the sun's light takes about eight minutes to reach you? When you look up at the sky you are actually looking right into the past. What you see happened eight minutes ago. If you can see the stars, which are much, much further away, it could also be many years ago.

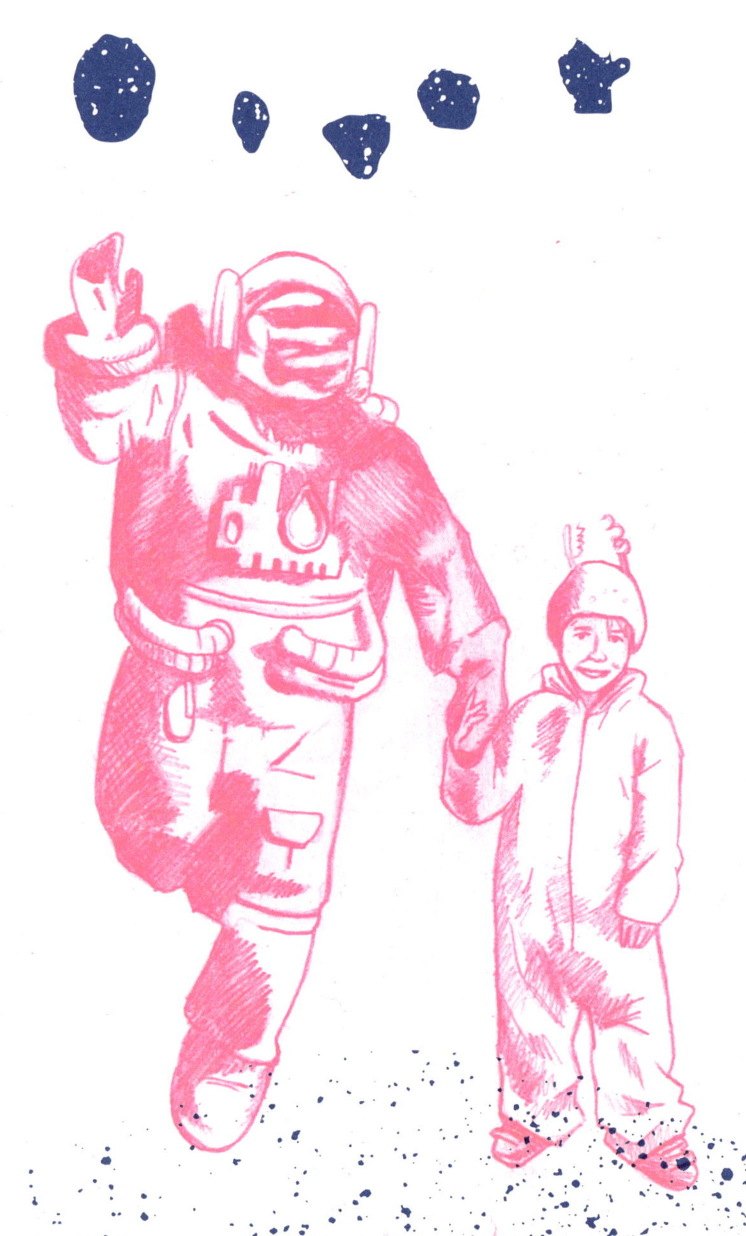

4. Do you know where the sun rises in the morning and where it sets in the evening? Turn and lie with your feet facing towards the sunrise. You probably know that it's not actually the sun that moves across the sky. Instead, the Earth spins, with you on it, like a merry-go-round.

And incredibly fast.

Right now, you are hurtling around the corner with the earth toward your feet, as the earth is turning at 1,660 kilometers per hour. Psst, can you hear the sound the Earth makes as it spins? At the same time, the Earth orbits the sun once a year at about 107,000 kilometers per hour. Much

faster

than any car or plane. Shoudn't we be wearing seat belts at such speed?

5. Exactly, and we are. Our seat belt is called gravity. Earth's gravity holds us tight. Try lifting your legs and holding them up for a moment. The fact that it's difficult isn't really because your legs are so heavy. In space, they don't weigh anything. Rather, it is the Earth's gravity that you feel. The Earth acts on us like a giant magnet. Luckily. If she didn't, we'd just be thrown out by the spin. Spaceship Earth keeps us safe in our gravity seat belt, while she is speeding with us through the

u n i v e r s e .

6. Now you can lower your legs again. Can you feel now—at least a little bit—how we fly while we are lying down? In a few hours you'll be pretty much where China is now. Would you like to wait for that?

Of course, not all children want to be astronauts. What would you like to be?

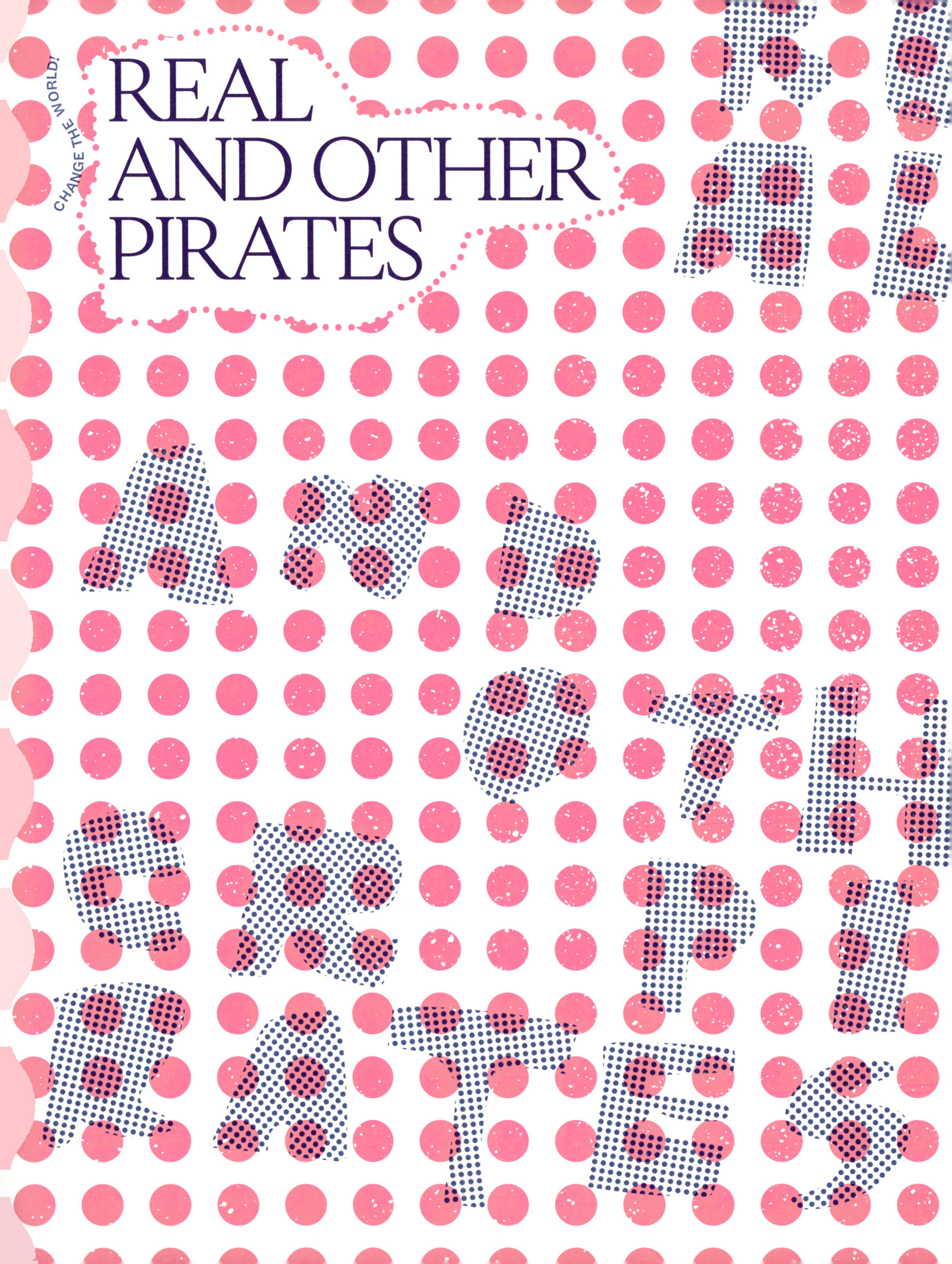
CHANGE THE WORLD!
REAL
AND OTHER
PIRATES

In our city many children like to be pirates. At least, they like to play pirates: They go on treasure hunts for their birthdays, they wave flags with skulls on them and wear eye patches. They also read tons of books and watch movies about pirates. When, without warning, real pirates came to our city, the children were very surprised: *How did the pirates come from the movies and the books into our world?* And: *Why does nobody seem to like the real pirates?*

How are reality and play connected when it comes to piracy? The children had many interesting questions about this. We invited them to wear their pirate costumes and recorded what they wanted to ask the real pirates on video. The pirates were from Somalia and were arrested for trying to hijack a ship from our city. Unfortunately, they weren't allowed to talk to us, as they were on trial. So, we had to find other real Somali pirates who could answer the children's questions. But how?

There is a theory that says that every human being on Earth is connected to every other human by six other human beings at most. The theory is called Six Degrees of Separation and it means: You know someone and they know someone and they know someone and they know someone and they know someone and they know Cristiano Ronaldo or Billie Eilish or a real pirate. We tried that and indeed: A friend knew someone and that person knew a scientist who was in Somalia for field research, and that person knew someone in Kenya and that person actually knew many Somali pirates.

One person from the pirates' organization was our contact. He spoke English, translated for us, and helped us to

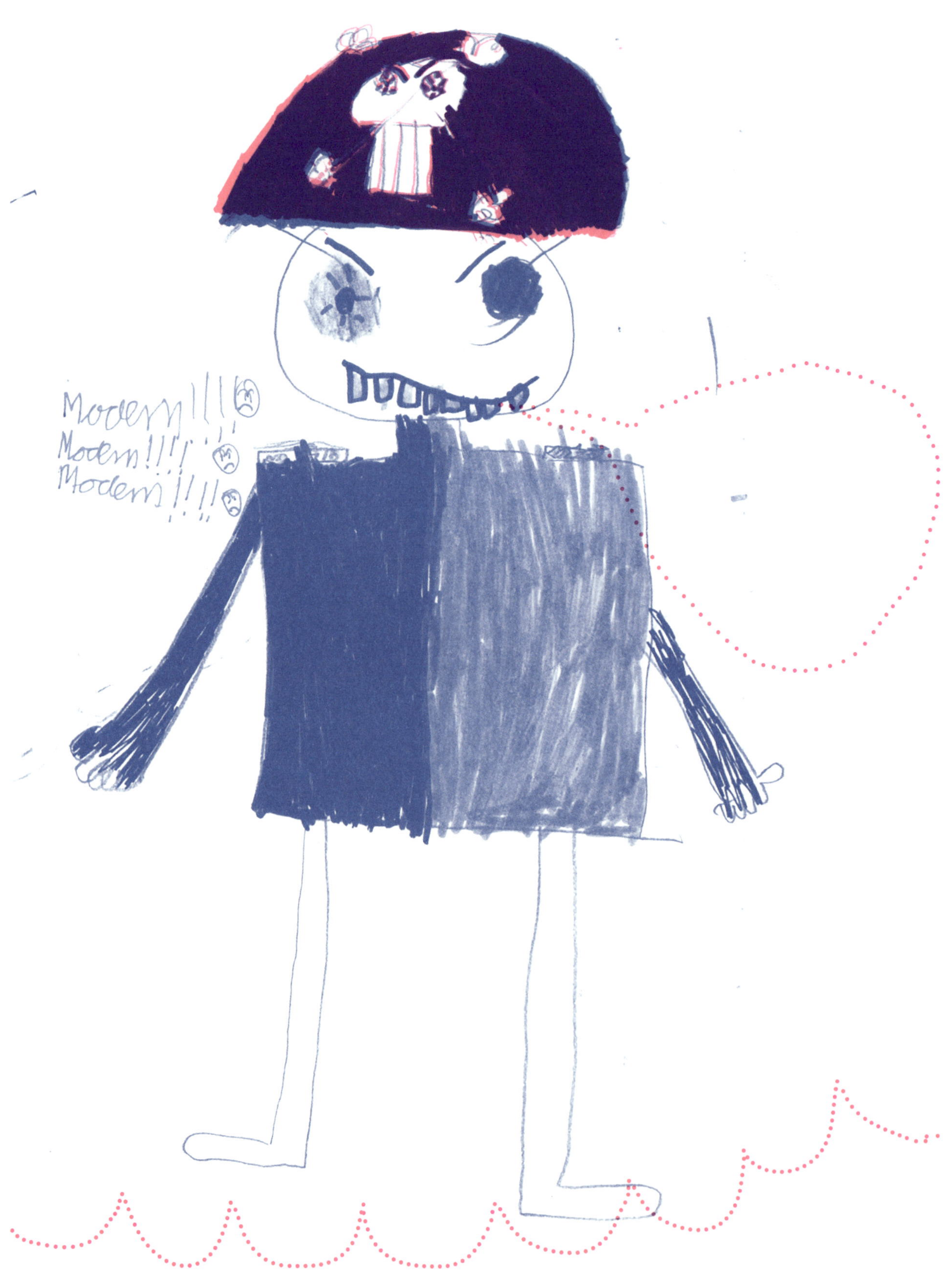
Modern!!!
Modern!!!
Modern!!!

determine if the people we interviewed actually were former pirates. We paid him and the other pirates for their time. Back then, Theatre of Research was co-funded by the maritime industry of Hamburg. To use that money for research on piracy felt right.

To tell you the truth: To try and find Somali pirates ready for an interview was a very long shot. We were surprised, and very nervous, when it actually worked. We traveled to Kenya, which is right next to Somalia, and met with the pirates. We sat with them in a hotel room and everyone there was a bit scared. We were scared of the pirates and they were scared of us. But then we showed them the videos with the children's questions and suddenly all the fear was gone. Sometimes you just need clever children in pirate costumes for adults to relax and speak openly.

What would you like to ask a real pirate?

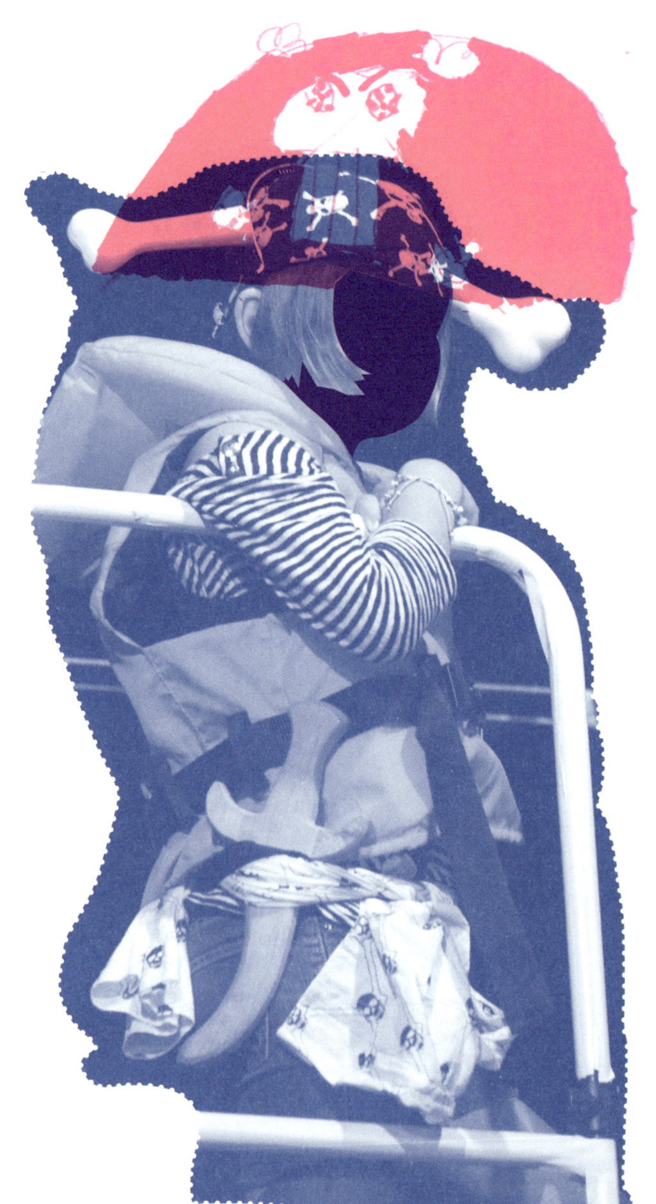

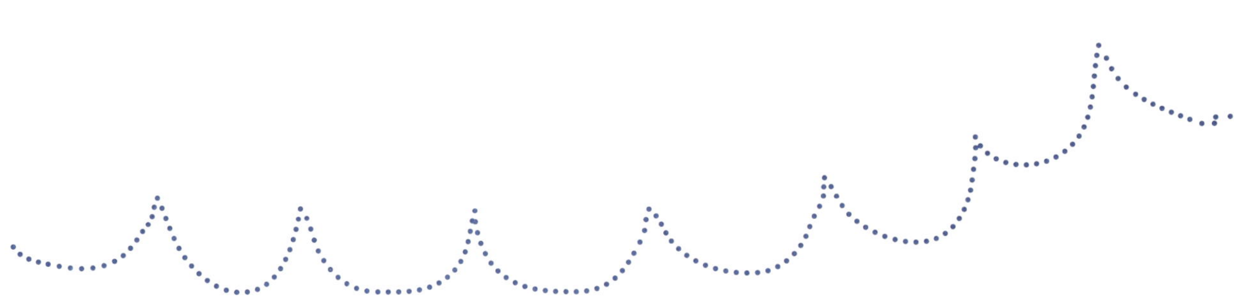

In our interviews we included questions from about sixty children and we talked to ten of the pirates. Some of them were old, some were young. Some had been successful pirates, most of them less so. On the next pages you will find a few questions from different children and a few answers from different pirates.

You can check whether your question is included, but beware: The life of a pirate can be sad and frightening. Don't say afterwards that we didn't warn you!

Q. When I play pirates I enjoy fighting and killing and getting all the money in the end. Is the real pirate life fun, too?

A. It's a difficult life. On the one hand you have the money, but on the other hand you can't eat anything all day, because you're always afraid.

Q. What exactly do you do as pirates ?

A. The pirates who want to attack the ship go to the ship in their boat. Some climb onto the ship, others stay in the boat. Once they have taken control of the ship and the crew, they will contact their people on land. The pirates then remain on the ship for at least two weeks until a ransom is paid.

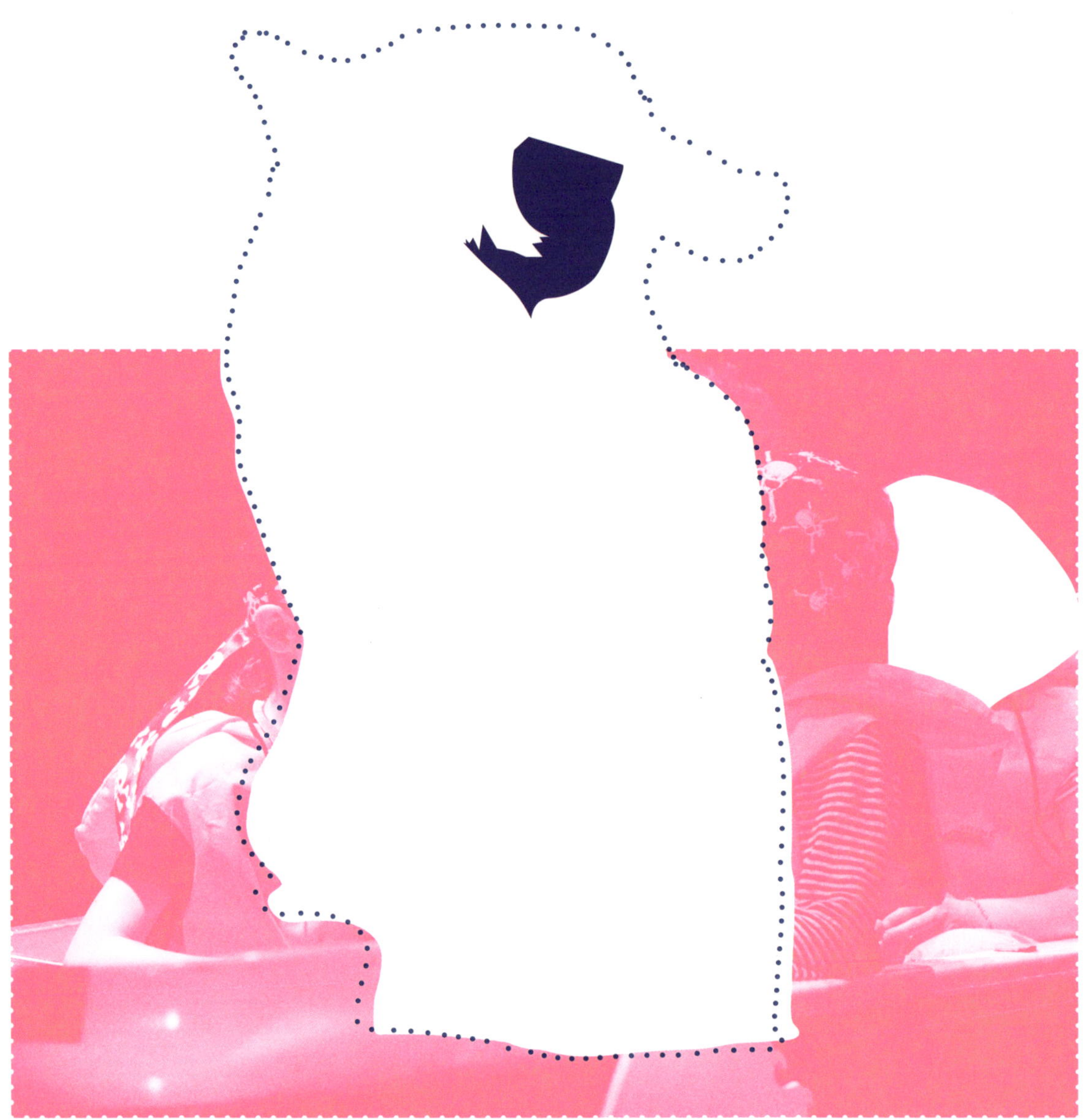

Q. How did you become a pirate in the first place?

A. My uncle had a boat. He was a fisherman. Then the boat broke and the net was destroyed by large ships. When the big ships of the fishing companies met the small boats of the Somali fishermen, they shot at the fishermen with hot water from pressure pumps. After this happened several times, we fishermen got together and decided that we have to fight back against these people who are destroying our nets. Also, we see the big ships as our enemies because they dump toxic chemicals into the sea. We experienced something like this ourselves: One night we were sleeping and when we woke up in the morning all the birds and all the fish in the sea were dead. A lot of people are getting sick in our country lately. We fear that Somalia has become the dumping ground for the rest of the world.

Q. Do you know *Pirates of the Caribbean*?

A. We'd rather watch James Bond.

Q. How old do you have to be to become a pirate?

A. Once you can carry a weapon, you can go to the pirates. If you're ten years old and you can carry a gun—

then go.

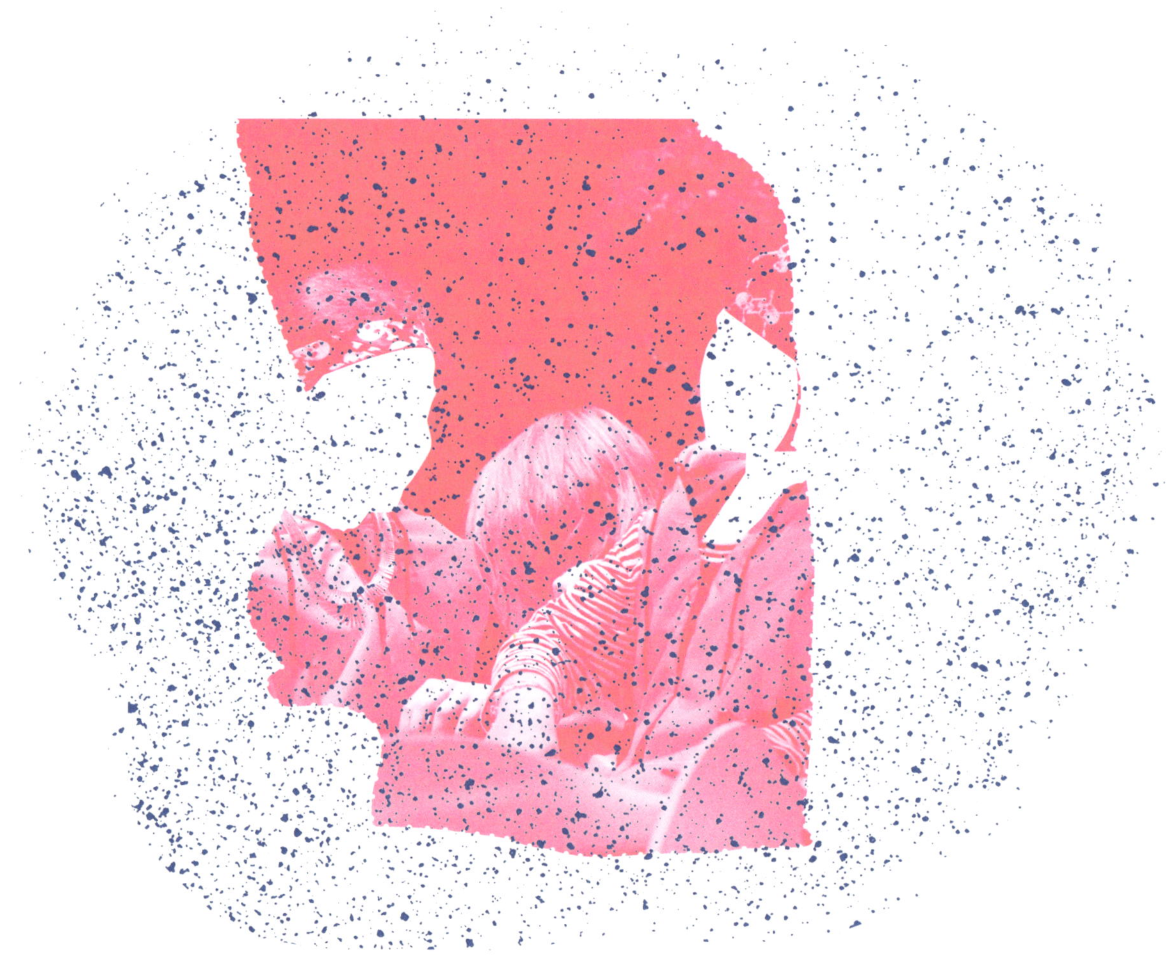

Q. Why do people from Europe come to Somalia to fish?

A. They come to us because there is no government and no laws in Somalia. They can take

all

the fish they want.

If there was a government and laws, there would be no pirates either.

Q. How many ships did you raid and how much money did you loot?

A. When I was with the pirates, I hijacked one ship. I was the youngest and didn't know much about piracy. That's why I told them I'll take what you want to give me. They gave me $15,000. Then I decided to leave piracy. On the way I was attacked by land pirates. They took the money away from me again.

Q. How does it feel when you get all the bling?

A. You feel like your team is winning the championship.

Q. Have you ever killed someone and doesn't that hurt you in your heart?

A. If you climb up there on the ship with your weapon, you say: *Hands up, surrender, sit on the ground.* It's not about killing people, it's just about the work. In my pirate group,

yes, people were killed there. And it makes me feel bad. But lately many pirates have been killed in the fight for the ships, too.

Q. Are you more scared, or do you feel more brave?

A. The men who go to sea are mostly very young. They can't read or write, they have nothing to lose. They are brave because their life is worth nothing to them.

Q. Do you share the ransom equally?

A. There is a point system. For example, the one who gives money to the pirates at the beginning, the investor, gets a high score. Or the one who provides the weapons, the boat or the ladder. There are points for everything. And according to the number of points, the loot is distributed. I had nothing but myself. That doesn't add up to so many points.

Q. Why can't the shipowners and the pirates sit down and negotiate – the pirates and those who catch the fish and those who throw the toxic waste into the sea?

A. This is not possible. Those who should sit around the table are the United Nations, the Somali government, and

the governments of the countries where the fishing companies come from. They must stop this predatory fishing.

Q. When you are old and have grandchildren one day, what **pirate** story will you tell them?

A. I will say: *Once upon a time, when I was your age or a little older, I was a pirate.* Then the children will ask me: *What is a pirate?* And I will say: *A pirate is someone who has a gun and sails the seas looking for ships to hijack.* And I will tell them: *I was once a fisherman with a little boat. Then a big ship came and destroyed my net. Back then we didn't have a government to protect our sea. Then I got angry and went to the pirates. We teamed up, attacked one of the big ships and captured it. There were white people on the ship, not like me. We didn't speak the same language and didn't understand each other. But then I felt that we are all the same, even if we don't speak the same language or have the same skin color. We are all human and I must respect and protect them.*

Q. If one of your children decided that they would want to become a pirate, what would you do then?

A. I would forbid that, I would not let my child go.

To be honest, the children in Hamburg were a bit disappointed by the pirates' answers, because the real pirates

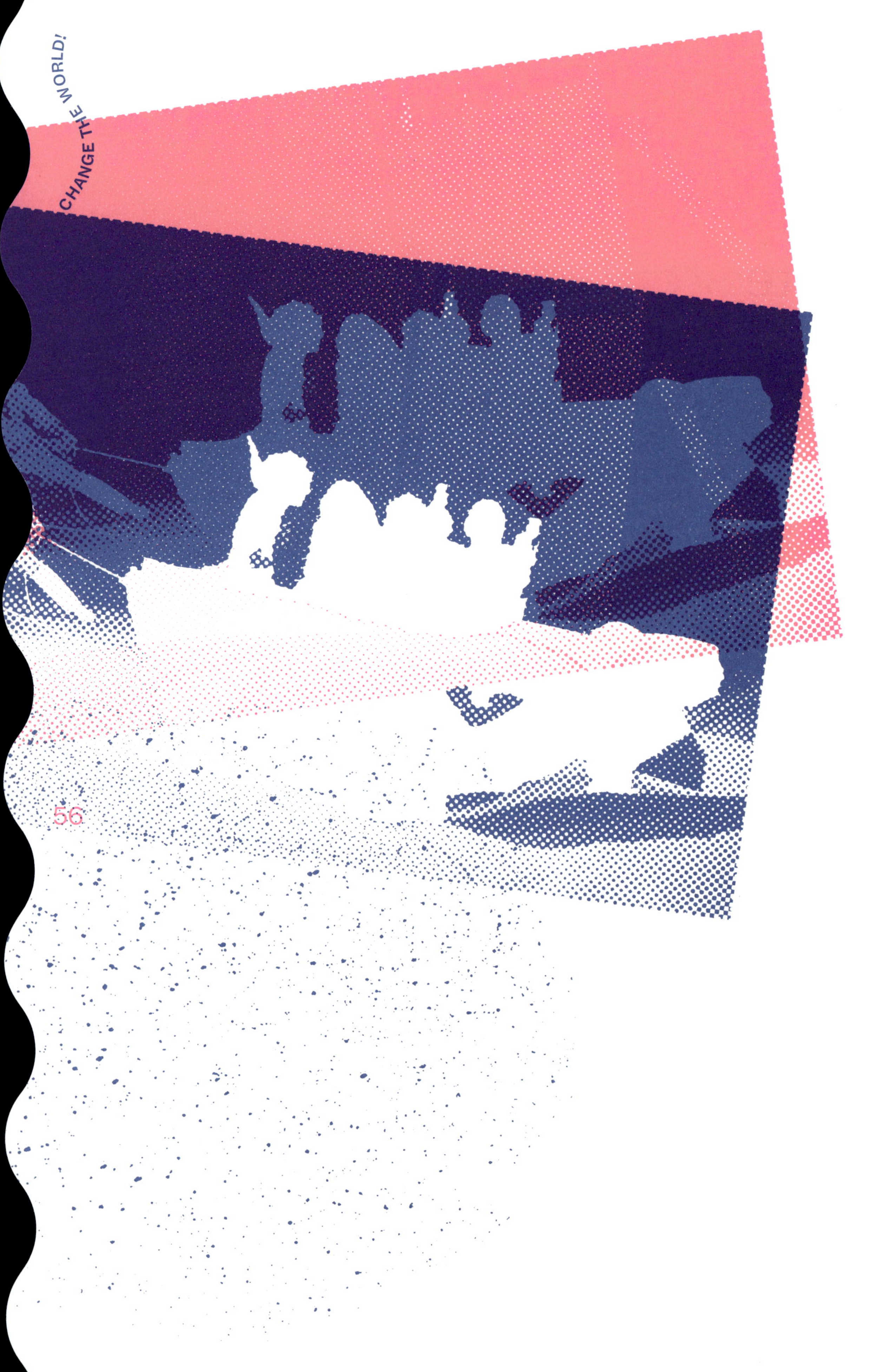

didn't think the pirate life was great, at all. Nevertheless, we all had goosebumps when we first showed the videos with the children's questions and the pirates' answers at Theatre of Research.[5] We learned a lot about Somali piracy.

With pirates, you can never be sure if they are freedom fighters or gangsters. They're both. Back when the famous pirates of the Caribbean roamed the seas, there was every reason to become a pirate. Many of the pirates had previously been slaves or marine soldiers who had been badly mistreated. Around 350 years ago, during the golden age of piracy, runaways from Europe, Africa and America met as equals at sea. They were the first who made democratic rules for their ships. According to these pirate rules, the captain was elected by the council of all pirates, and everyone got an equal share of everything. There was also insurance, if pirates got injured. The pirates from our city, who lived some 600 years ago, were similar. They called themselves the Likkedeelers, which translates as equal sharers.

The Somali pirates don't share equally. Nevertheless, they, too, had good reasons to rebel against the big fishing companies from the rich countries. The world of Somali pirates is completely different than life in our city, and it doesn't usually happen that children from Europe and Somali pirates talk to each other. Play and reality met and created an improbable connection. We will never forget it.

There are not just pirates in play AND in reality. There are also witches and

5 Once again, Theatre of Research teamed up with Secret Agency for this project, which was initially called Parléz. After the research process in 2011, the outcomes were presented as a performance called *Real and Other Pirates*, first in 2012 at Theatre of Research. Then it travelled to Vienna and Berlin.

princesses. For example, the witch Starhawk from California or the Princess Senate Seeiso from Lesotho, do you know them? We've long wanted to collect questions from kids for real witches or princesses and send them to Starhawk and Senate. How would play and reality meet then? Unfortunately, we haven't had time to do that, yet. Maybe you want to have a go?

Your questions for witches and princesses:

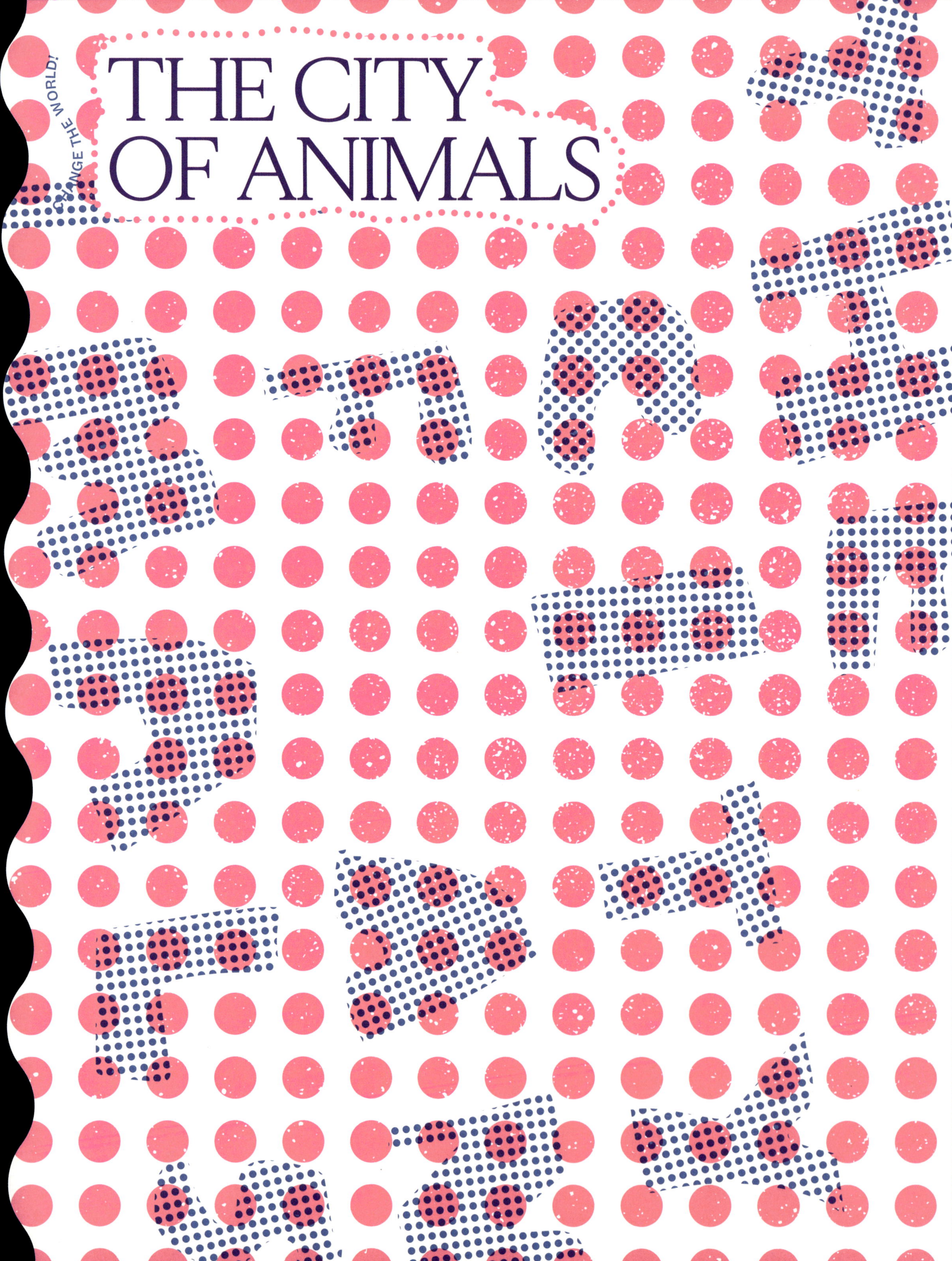
CHANGE THE WORLD!
THE CITY
OF ANIMALS

A few years ago, we appointed children directors of Theatre of Research and gave them suitcases with 1,000 euros in each of them: Who or what would the children like to book and invite to the stage?

The children then booked lots of animal acts. Dogs, spiders, chickens, rabbits and even almost real unicorns were the new stars in our theater. We, the adults, didn't like that much at first. We asked: *Can't you go to the zoo or the circus if you want to see animals?* But the children said: *In the zoo and in the circus, the animals are forced and caged. But we want to be friends with them. We almost never meet animals, we miss them!* That was true: All small children get to know about farm animals and their different voices. But they almost never see them in real life, except for maybe a cow from afar once in a while.

So,
where
did
all
the
animals
go?

In a report by the United Nations, we read that of all mammals on Earth, only four percent are still wild animals, that is four out of one hundred! By far the most mammals on earth are bred and kept and eaten by humans.

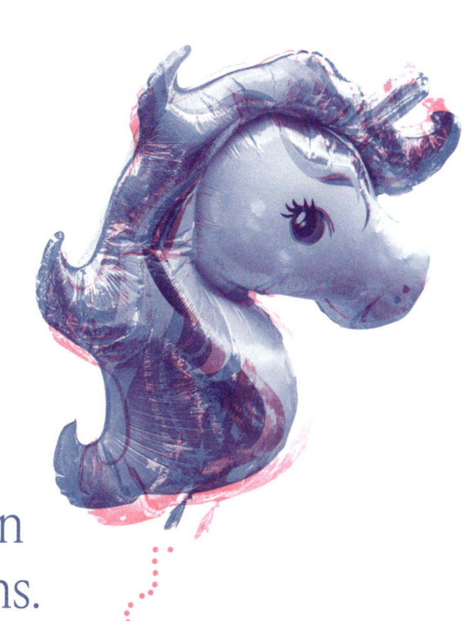

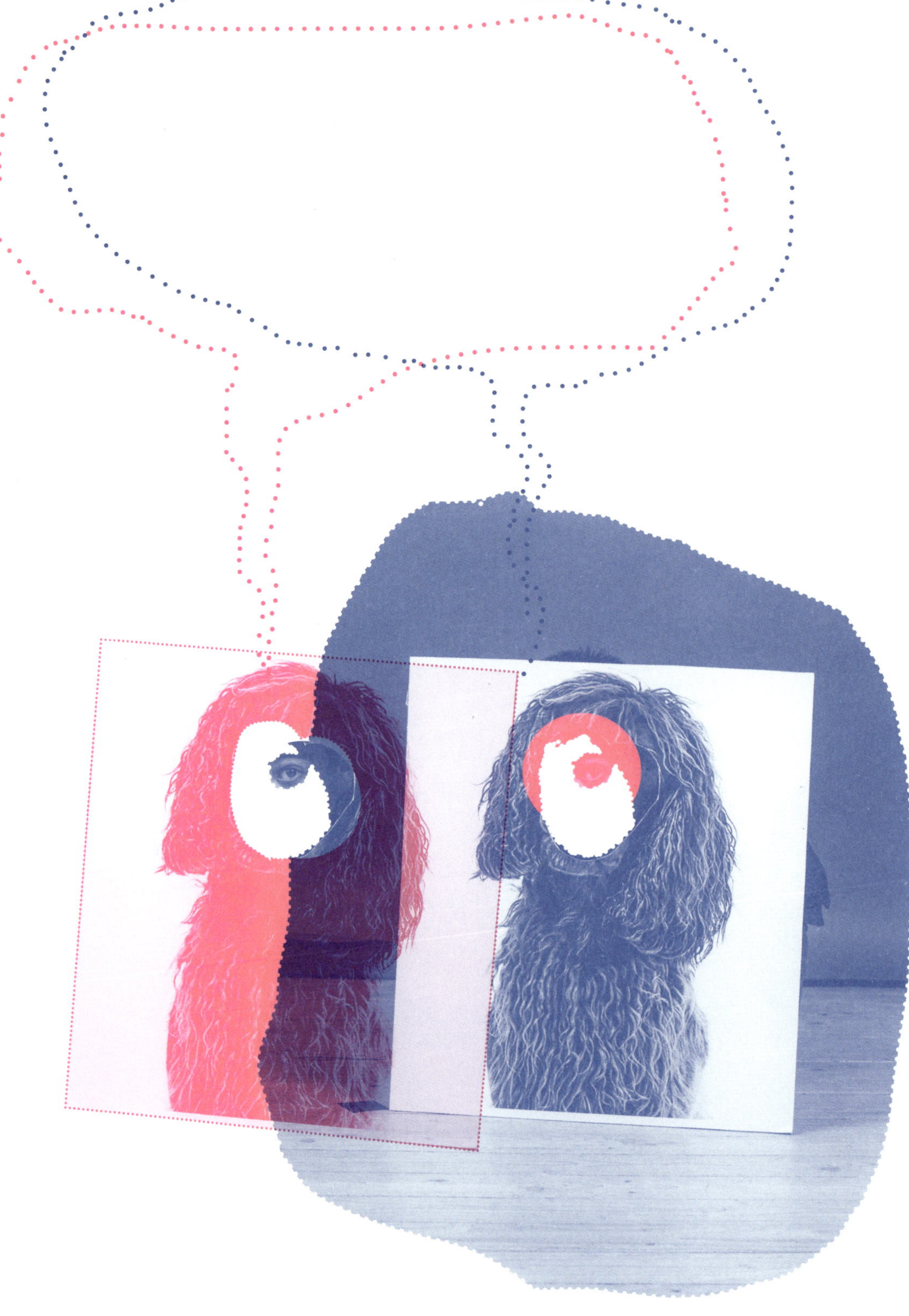

Strangely, we hardly ever see them either, because most of them live in factory stables without a chance to ever leave. Befriending animals is difficult because we rarely ever meet animals as equals. For a long time, humans thought they were completely different from all the other animals. Human philosophers took pride in pointing out differences between humans and other animals. For example, they said that only humans have free will, while animals are controlled by instincts. They said only humans have language, and animals don't. Children always had their doubts about this. But lately there are more and more adults who question this order of things, too. We know by now that animals have language and free will. More importantly, it doesn't seem smart to think about humans being so much better than all the other species on this planet. Instead, it becomes clear that we are in this together for better or for worse. We are not one species winning the food chain game. Rather, we are a companion species dependent on others. However, in the industrialized parts of the world, we have not ordered life this way. How could we change the order between humans and non-humans?

To find out, Theatre of Research founded the City of Animals. The City of Animals was really a park. For a little while we turned it into a city where all animals, including humans, should have equal rights. Many children, artists, researchers, people, and non-human animals invented, planned, and finally made the City of Animals a reality.[6]

6 The first City of Animals was called Animals of Manchester (including humans). We realized it together in summer 2019 with Lois Keidan from the Live Art Development Agency, Manchester International Festival, and many other artists and children

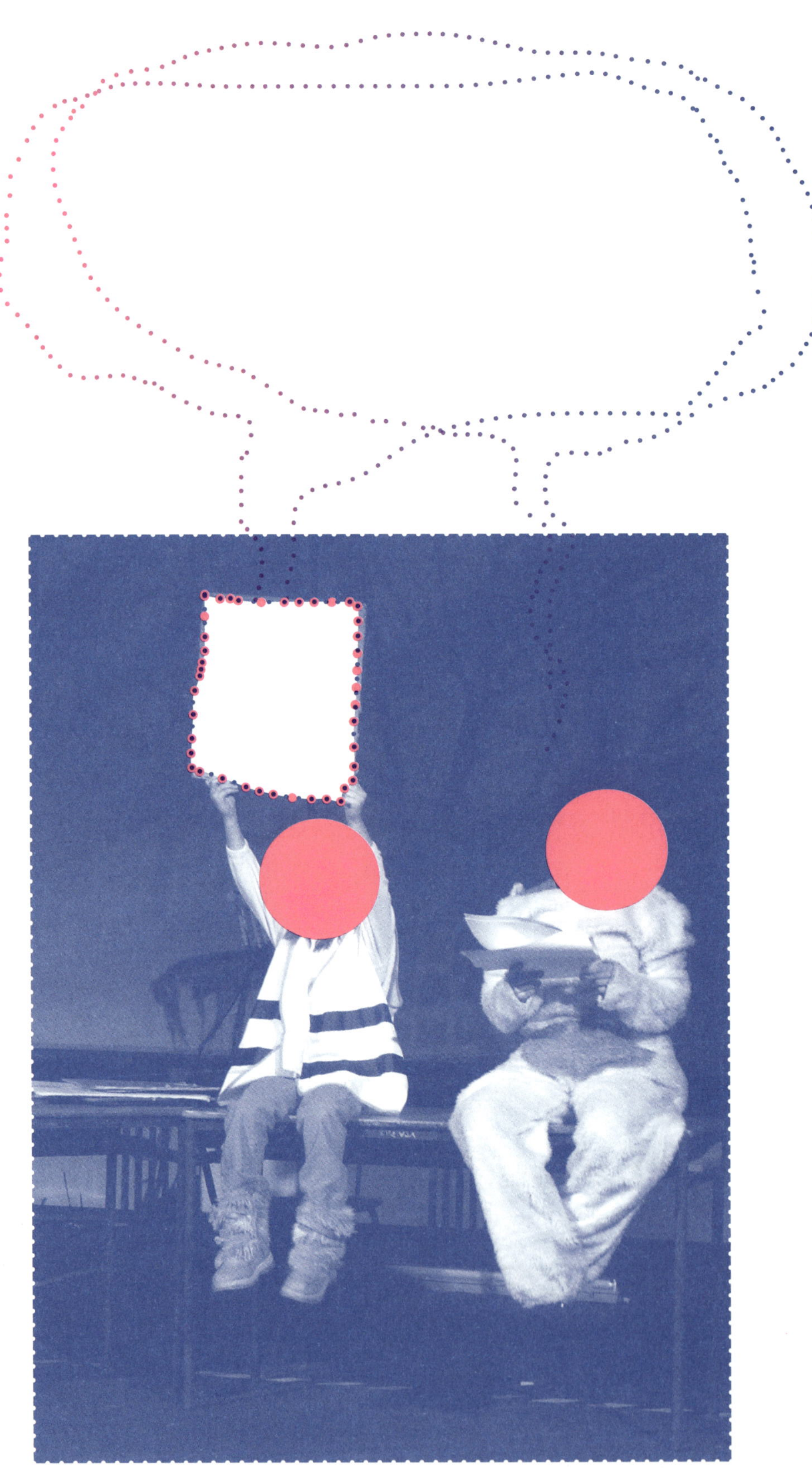

IF YOU ALSO WOULD LIKE TO CREATE ONE, HERE IS HOW:

1. Find an outdoor area that is to become the City of Animals. Who owns it? What are the rules here? In dealing with these rules you might learn a lot about how far apart play and reality actually are in regard to humans and other animals.

2. Find out which animals live at the site or use it in some way: Birds? Insects? Rodents? Observe them carefully and respectfully. What is the relationship between humans and other animals on the site? How could it be changed in favor of nonhuman animals? How could they be invited onto the land? What do they need that could be made available here? Are there pets present in the space? What is the relationship between humans and their pets and how could it become more equal?

3. Make the agency of nonhuman animals more tangible for humans: how can nonhuman animals be empowered and put in charge? For example: Set up a dance school in which dogs are the lead dancers and everyone else has to follow their movements.

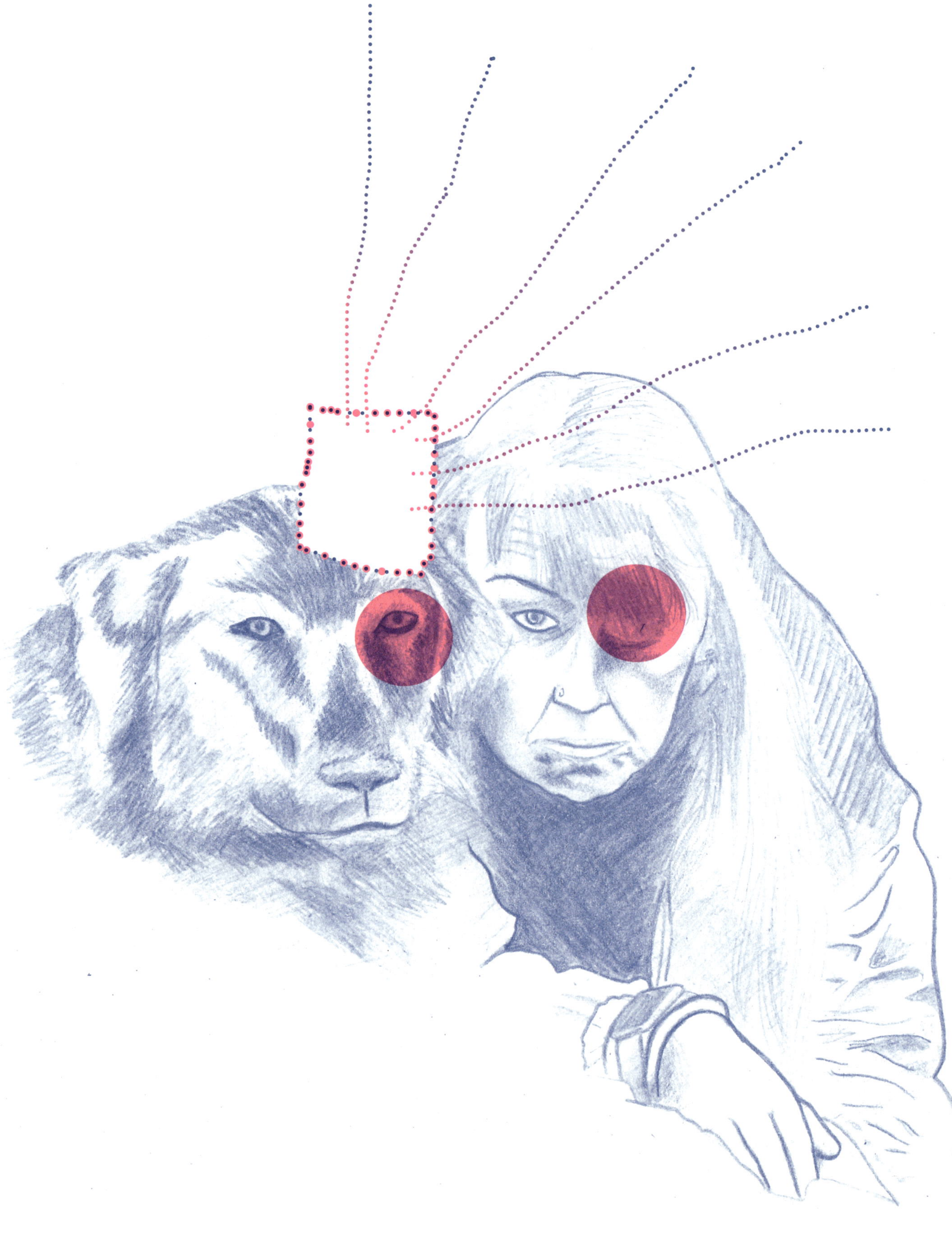

4. What is the relationship between humans and other animals in the neighborhood? Go to the nearest supermarket. How many animal products can you find in the supermarket? What do you know about how they get to the supermarket and where and how these animals actually live?

5. Find two living animals of a species found in the supermarket, which live close by and can be transported without stressing them too much. Give them a home in the City of Animals for a few days and make everybody get to know and admire them: cows, pigs, or maybe chickens? Appoint them as mayors of the city. How do they behave? How could their behavior become some kind of decision-making power? Warning: These animals need care and protection. A person who knows these animals well must look after them at all times.

6. Hold a ritual in which all humans who have participated in the process become citizens of the City of Animals—animals among animals, who renounce their human privileges. Now other people can be invited to the City of Animals. The participating kids can guide them through the site and let them experience for themselves what is different here. Then they can also become citizens of the city, animals among animals.

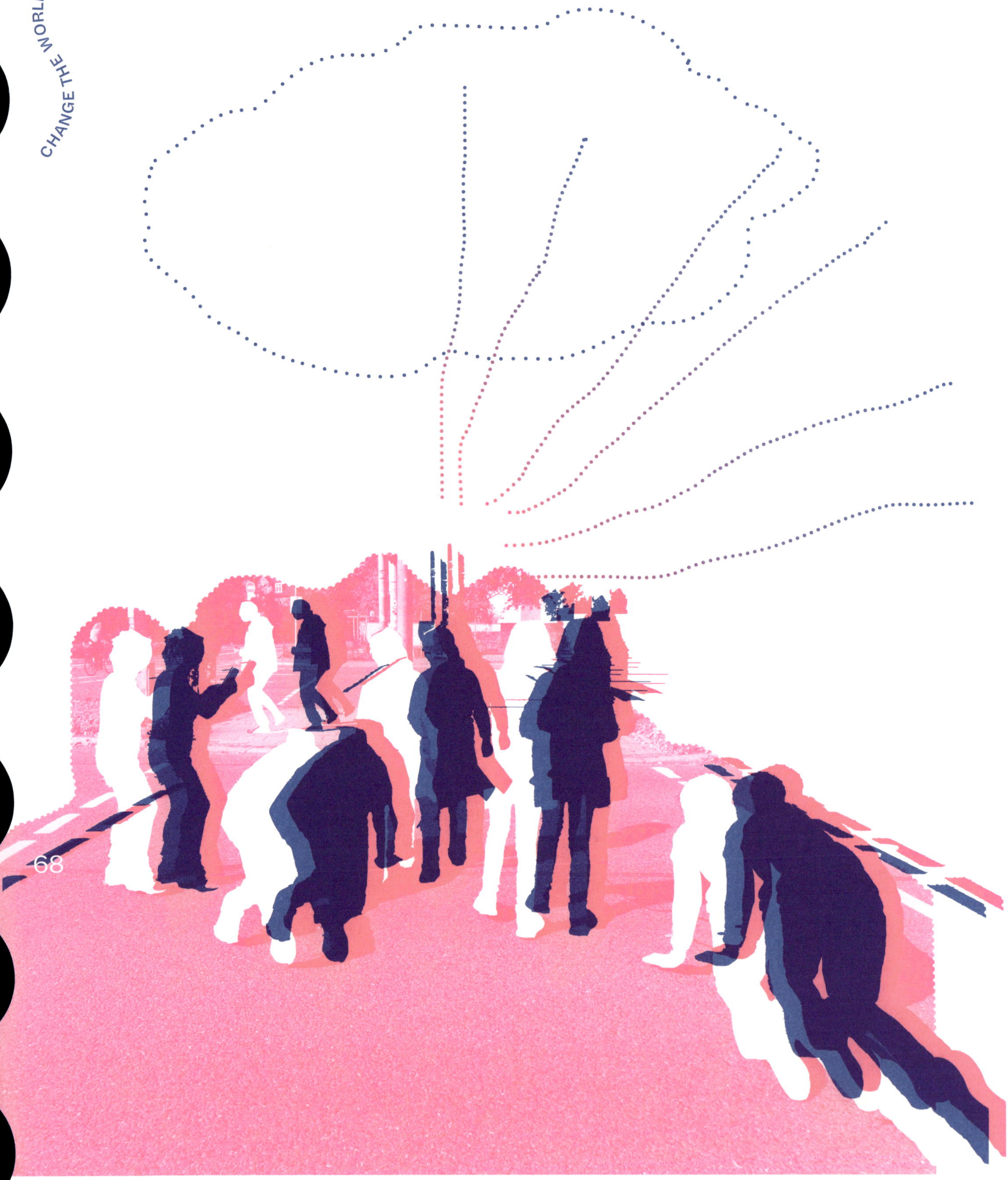

7. Record everything you have discovered in the development of the City of Animals. Do you have any suggestions on how the overall relationship between humans and other animals could be improved? And one last question. What do you think: Is the City of Animals a work of art? And can nonhuman animals also be artists?

In the first City of Animals, we appointed the cows Pandora and Petul as the mayors of our city. As they were in charge, the meetings in the open air townhall could only take place if the two came out of their stable. Around the townhall a lot of other things were going on: Baby hedgehogs, whose mothers had been killed by lawnmowers, were fed and looked after at the Hedgehog Hospital. A tiny town made entirely of nuts was built for the squirrels. In the Forest of Extinct Species, kids and adults wrote poetry from the point of view of saber-toothed tigers. There was a museum inside the City of Animals in which animals were honored as artists. In the Beetle Film Theatre, the beetles appeared voluntarily on the film set. And there even was a school for humans, in which dogs were the teachers.[7]

Many children and adults registered as new citizens of the city and promised to be animals among animals from now on. The City of Animals was a fantastic and very unlikely place. However, there were also difficulties: So many people came that the squirrels got scared. It also didn't suit

7 These are some of the the artists, activists, and organizations involved in the artworks mentioned above: Barbara Roberts, Rebecca Chesney and the Withington Hedgehog Care Trust, London Fieldworks, Marcus Coates and Adam O'Riordan, Tim Spooner, and Angela Bartram.

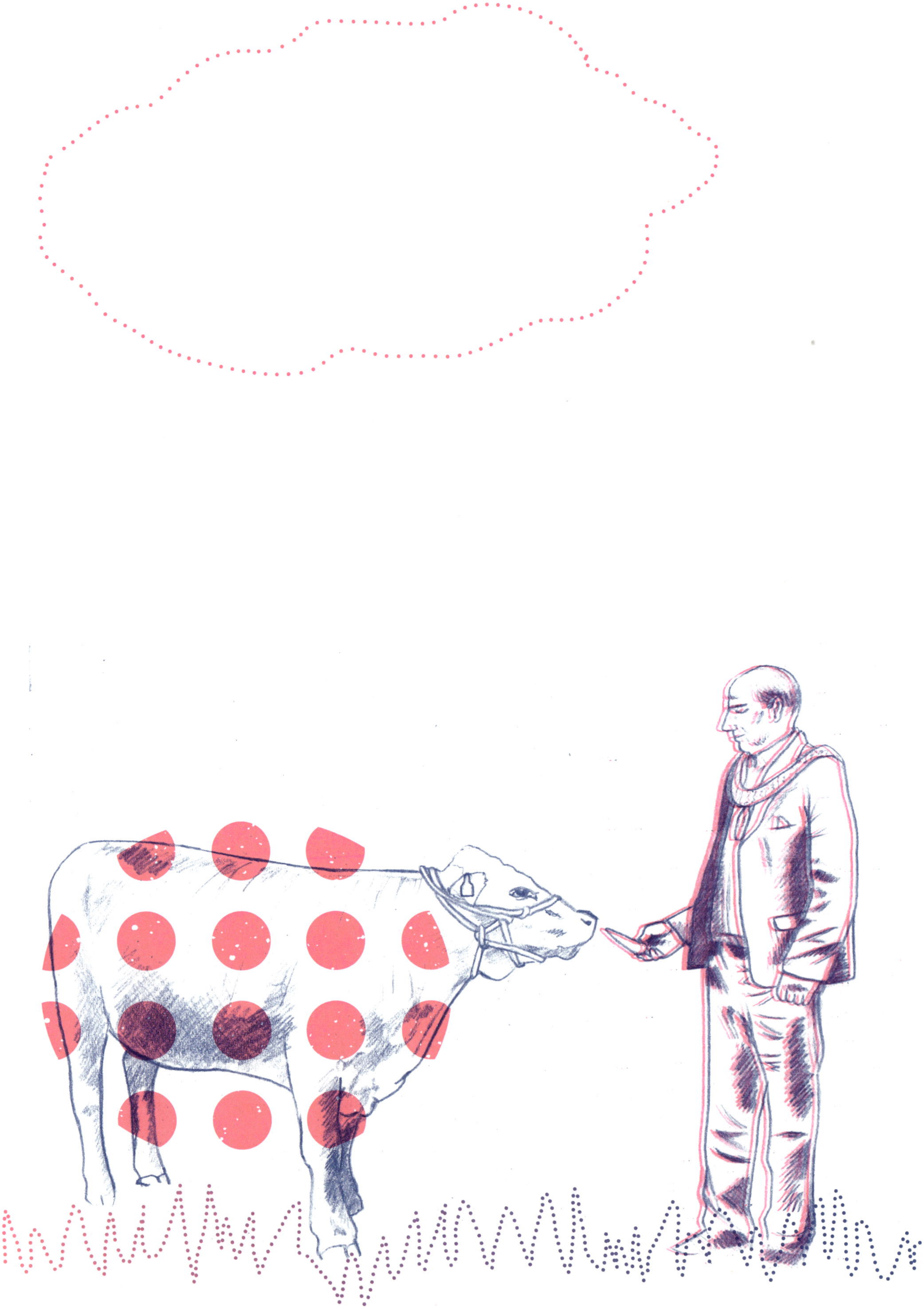

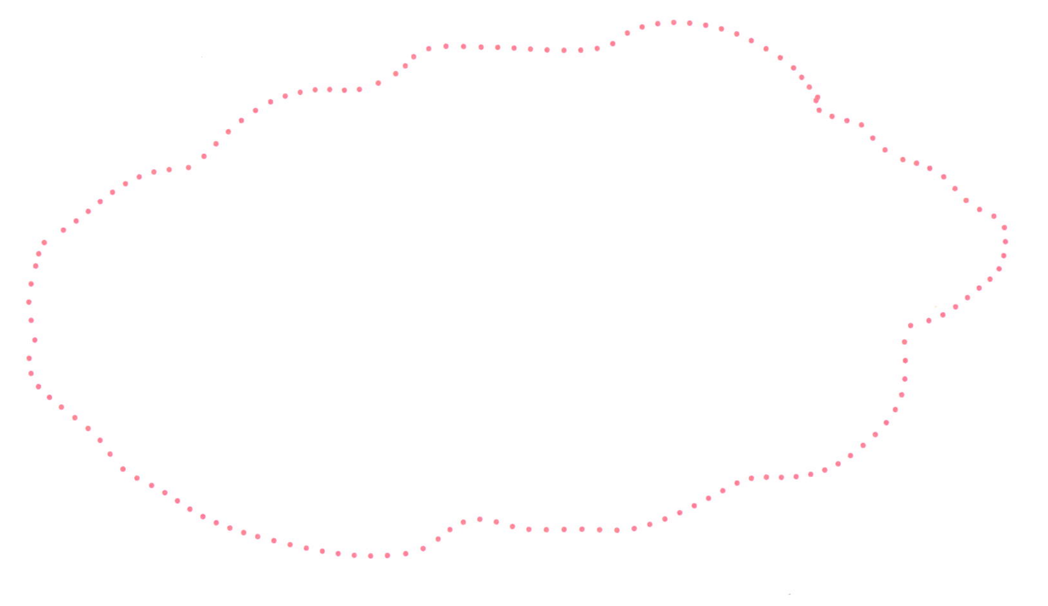

the City of Animals that all dogs had to be on a leash. So, we made new leashes that had belts on both sides so that dogs and people could walk on the leash together.

A few children became good friends with the cows Petul and Pandora.

They thought a lot about what humans and cows have in common.

At first, they thought that cows always give milk and that people only give milk when they have babies. But then they learned that cows and humans are the same in this respect and that the cows and their calves are usually separated from each other in the process. Some of the children knew the problem from their own lives—they also got separated from their parents. *You know what,* said one of the children, *I know one more thing people and cows have in common:*

people and cows—
both only have
one childhood.

Setting up a zone where different rules apply is a kind of research that takes place right on the edge between play and reality. It's about making the zone as real as possible: How do you make sure that different rules really apply here? And how does it feel to observe these other rules? Even if you don't quite make it to equality, you will learn a lot. Unfortunately, the City of Animals only existed for a few days. Just long enough to look forward to the next one.

Here you can draw a map of your City of Animals:

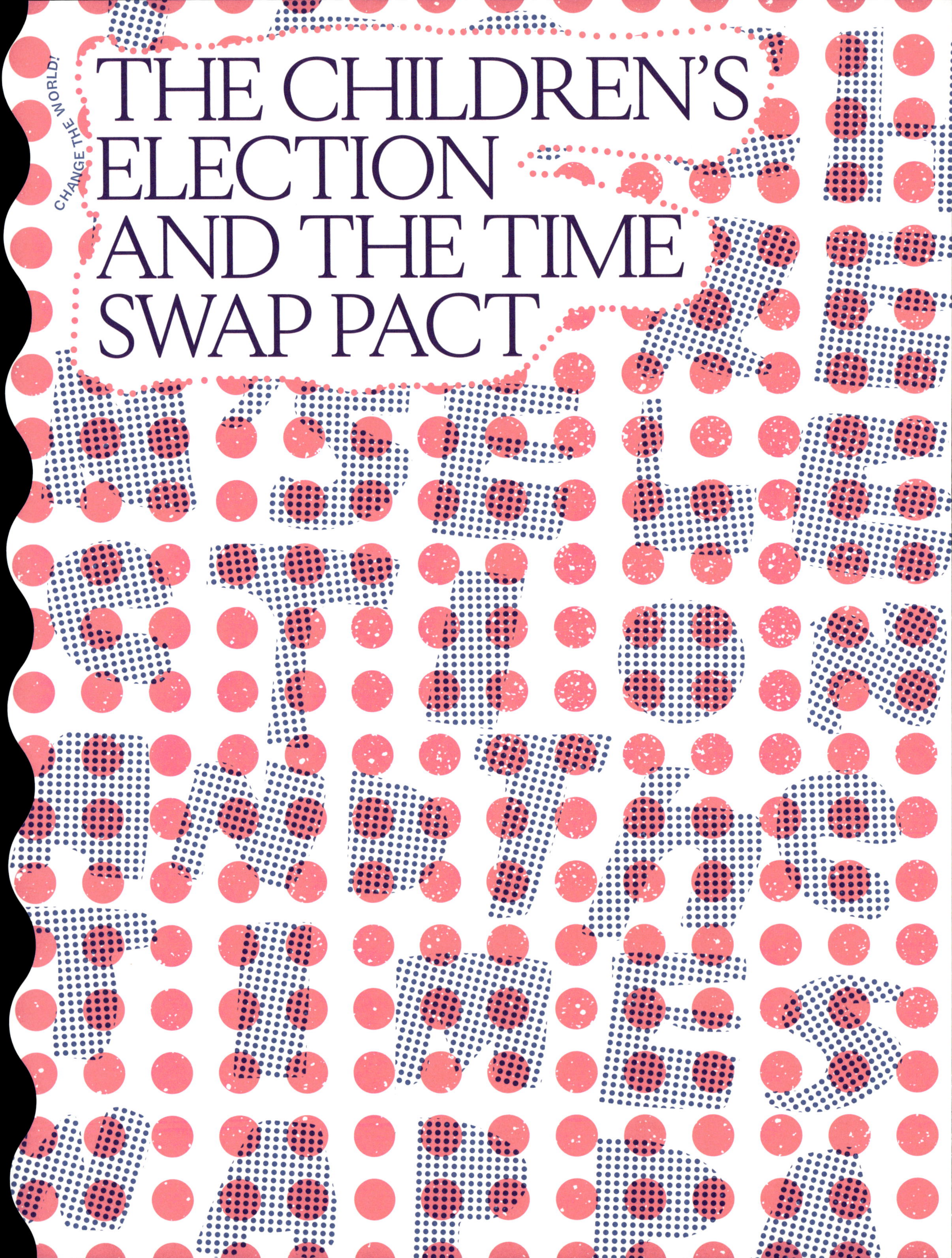

THE CHILDREN'S ELECTION AND THE TIME SWAP PACT

In the City of Animals, we learned something about humans and animals: that they are made into opposites to give people

power over animals.

To create opposites can often be part of a power play. For example, is the opposite children vs. adults also a power play? It puts adults in power over children, doesn't it?

In Theatre of Research, children and adults always do research together. We think research is better when lots of very different people are involved. At some point we asked ourselves why that works so well in our theater but apparently nowhere else? For example, in politics: Why are children not allowed to vote? If politicians would explain politics in such a way that children could understand it, many adults would also finally get the gist. Maybe even the politicians themselves would, too. That's why Theatre of Research opened an office for children to vote, where children could talk to politicians, find out about the political programs of the different parties, and vote for themselves.[8] In our Children's Election almost all the children voted for the political party that promised to really do something for the environment. To hold a children's election

8 The Children's Election was initiated, invented, and hosted by Hannah Kowalski and Christopher Weymann in 2020 as part of the elections for the city of Hamburg.

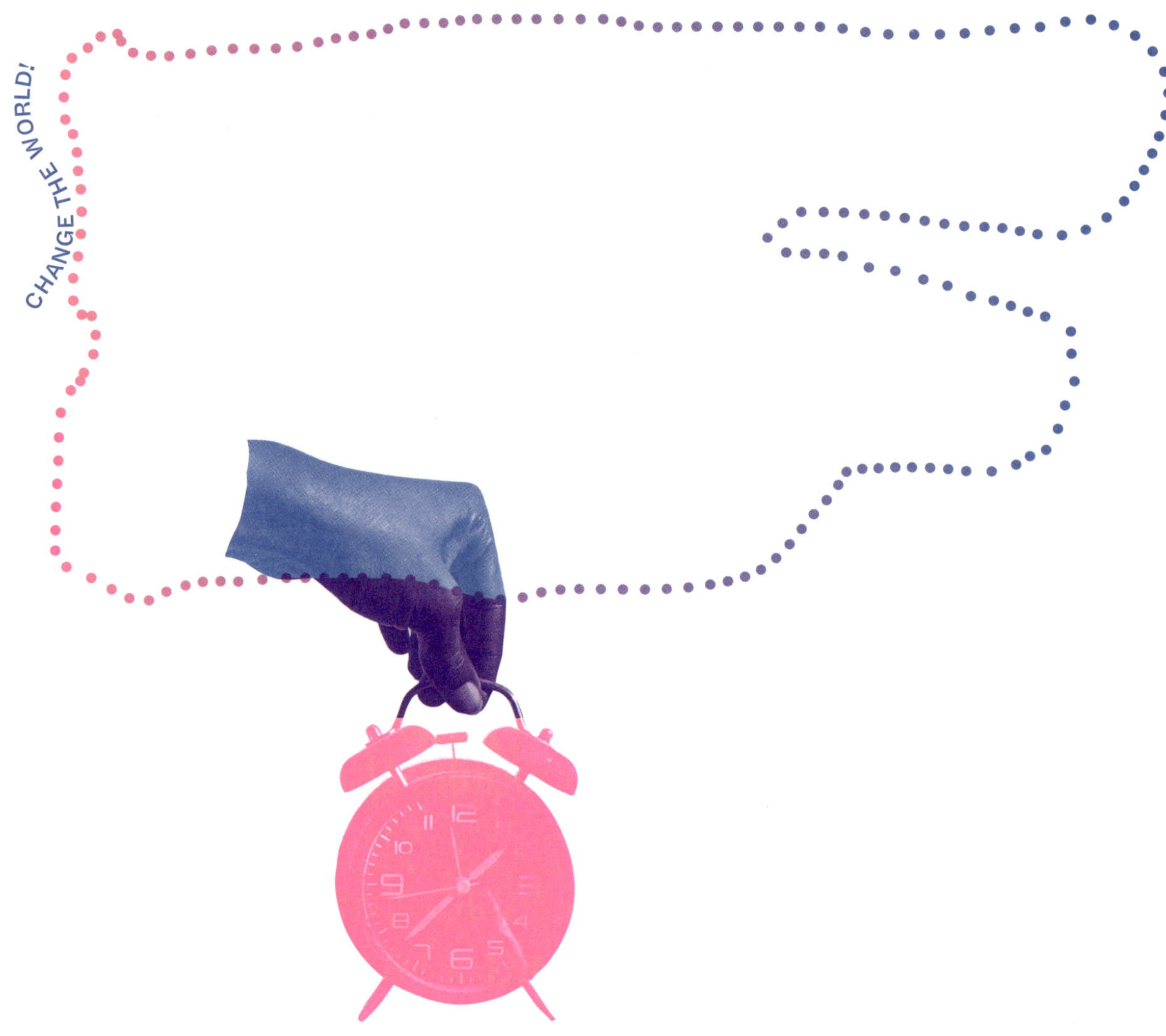
CHANGE THE WORLD!

like that, adults had to give their votes to children. That's not easy, because legally, votes are not transferrable. Therefore, we invited families to let the children decide their parents' vote. Maybe in the next election you could decide what to vote for together with your parents, too?

Today's politics will have a major impact on life fifty years from now. Then many of the adults who make the decisions now will no longer be alive. The children, who are not allowed to have a say today, will have to live with the consequences. If you can't hold a children's election, there is another way to do something about that. We called it the Time Swap Pact.[9] In such a pact, children and older adults exchange one day of their lives with each other. The adults give up a day in the near future, next Friday, for example. And the children can decide what the adults should do on that day. For example, an adult had to lie on the roof of his car instead of driving it. Another one had to go to the public pool and discuss rising water levels while in the water. In return, the children promise the adults one day of their future, one day in fifty years. And the adults get to decide what the children should do on that distant day in the future, when the adults might not be around anymore. For example, the children, who will then no longer be children, will have to bake an apple pie according to Grandma's old recipe, or get to a certain place and sing a song there.

If you would also like to make a Time Swap Pact, you could swap a day with your grandparents!

9 We invented the Time Swap Pact together with Eva Plischke in 2010.

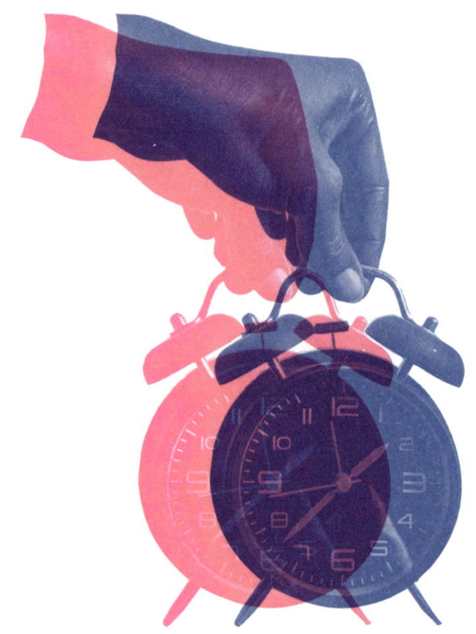

TIME SWAP PACT

Name..

and

Name..

commit to spending

the Day (Date)...................................

doing the following:

the Day (Date)...................................

doing the following:

Signatures

....

If you found a partner for your Time Swap Pact and have decided which days to swap and what to do on those days, you can invent and hold a celebratory ritual to seal the pact.

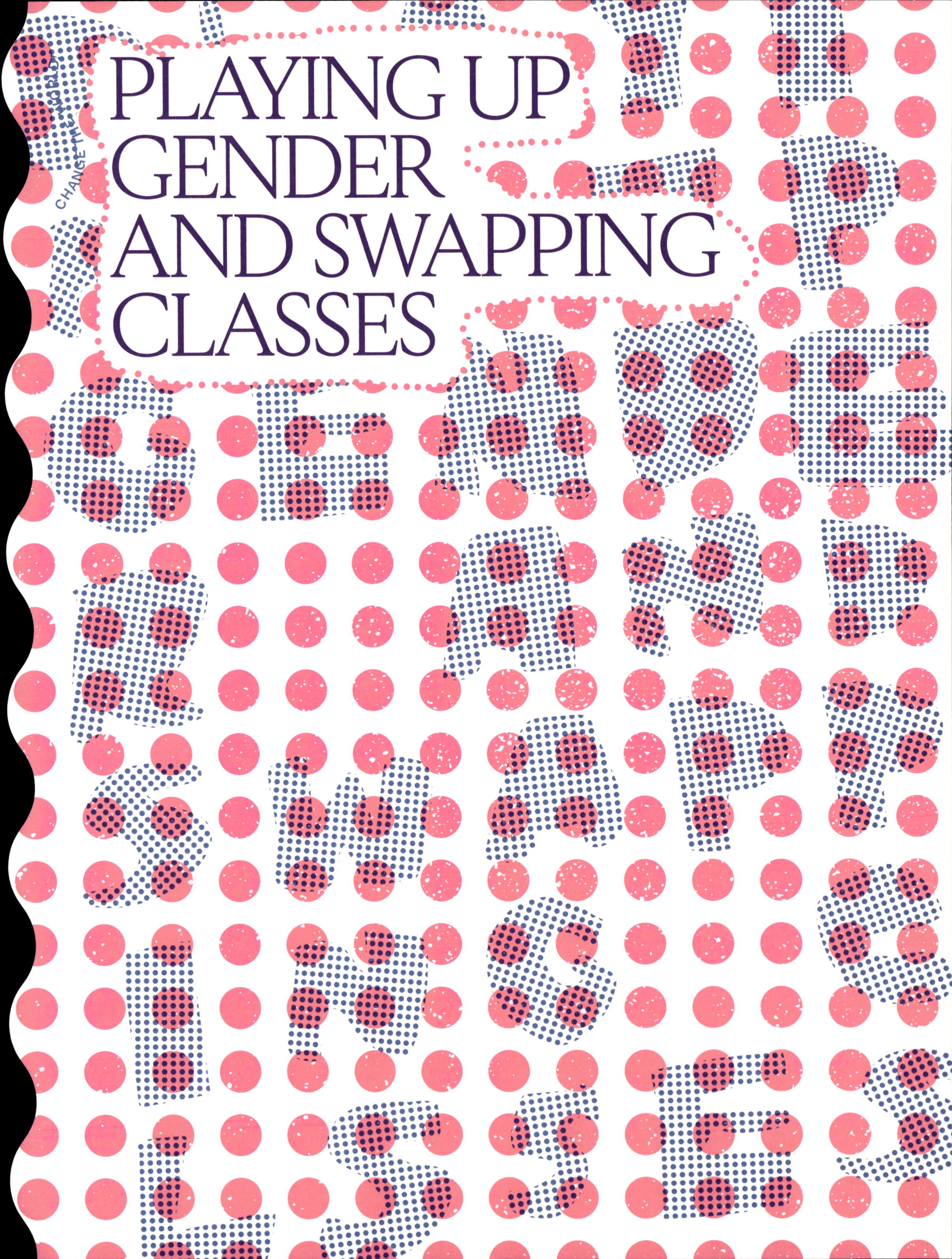

CHANGE THE WORLD
PLAYING UP GENDER AND SWAPPING CLASSES

In addition to children vs. adults and humans vs. animals, there are other similar opposites which also involve a power play. Men vs. women, for example. Even though we have legal gender equality in many countries today, this opposite gave men power over women for a very long time.

One problem with these opposites, which are actually power plays, is that they just don't fit: As you know, there are lots of children who are smarter and more responsible than adults. Also, there are lots of animals who have characteristics that were reserved for humans for the longest time. And there are a lot of people who do not fit on either side of the opposite man vs. woman, boy vs. girl. You probably know a few, too. In the end we might all be a bit boy and a bit girl—in a unique mixture. That makes it annoying to always ask ourselves how we are supposed to be and act as a "boy" or a "girl." It's much nicer when we don't have to do, and be, either. In recent years, many young people have questioned whether we could overcome the opposite boys vs. girls. What do you think about that?

How would the world change if we nullified the gender opposites? What if we played the whole man-woman-boy-girl game differently or just didn't play it at all?

Here is an idea: In recent years artists have done exciting experiments to question the rules regarding what boys and girls, men and women allegedly are or how they are supposed to behave.[10] Theatre of Research has collected some of these experiments and added instructions for you to redo them yourself.

10 See gender.playingup.de/en/home.html

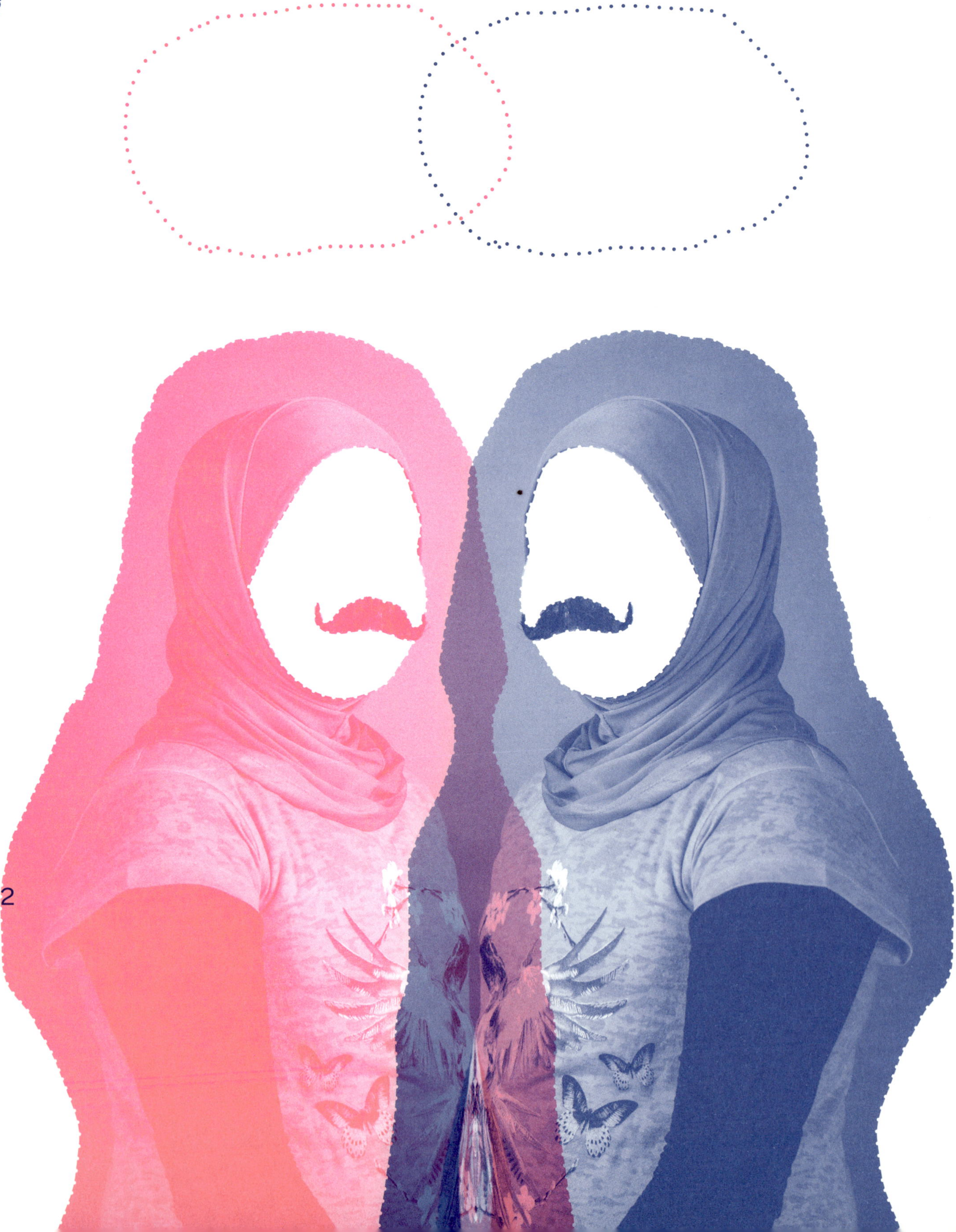

This takes the form of a game called Playing Up Gender. Lots of kids and adults had fun exploring it. Have a look yourself at gender.playingup.de!

Or would you like to try your own version? Imagine a day at school without gender opposites: What would have to change? The dress code, the toilets, names and pronouns—what else?

CHANGE THE WORLD!

And what would you do
on a day
without
the gender
opposites?

Why is the world divided into animals and humans, children and adults, men and women? Could it be different? Often it appears to be difficult, if not impossible, to change something about these divisions. But by doing research between play and reality we can still change things. Maybe not forever and everywhere, but here and now. Do you know any other opposites which are actually power plays and divide the world in a bad way?

What about the opposite of rich vs. poor? We already talked about it in the chapter about The Children's Bank. Actually, the difference between the rich and the poor is becoming bigger and bigger these days. Our cities are divided into places for the rich and places for the poor. So rich and poor people often don't even meet.

As school classes from all parts of our city came to visit Theatre of Research, we saw a chance to change that and invented the Class Swap:[11] school classes from poor and rich parts of our city swapped their schools and free time activities for one day. The children from the different schools did not meet at first, instead they wrote travel guides for their school and their neighborhood to let the other kids know that there is a great tree for climbing behind the gym and that you better be careful around the headmaster's dog. Then they swapped classrooms, teachers, and the

11 We made Class Swap together with Esther Pilkington in 2014.

I didn't know playing a game could be art.
Oshin Biswas

afternoon program with each other for one day. The team from Theatre of Research documented the Class Swap: What did children think about the other school and the other neighborhood? What did they like, what not so much? What questions did they have about how people lived in the other neighborhood?

A few days later they came to Theatre of Research:

on
one side
of the
red curtain
sat
one group
of
kids

a n d

on
the other side
sat
the other.

Then the curtain went up and the two classes saw each other for the first time. They told each other about their journey into their everyday lives and got to know each other better. Interestingly, it turned out that the kids from one of the rich schools liked it better in the poorer neighborhood because there were so many collective activities there. In their own rich part of town, school ended much earlier and afternoons alone in big houses can be pretty boring and lonely.

Maybe you want to swap classes, too? We recommend it!

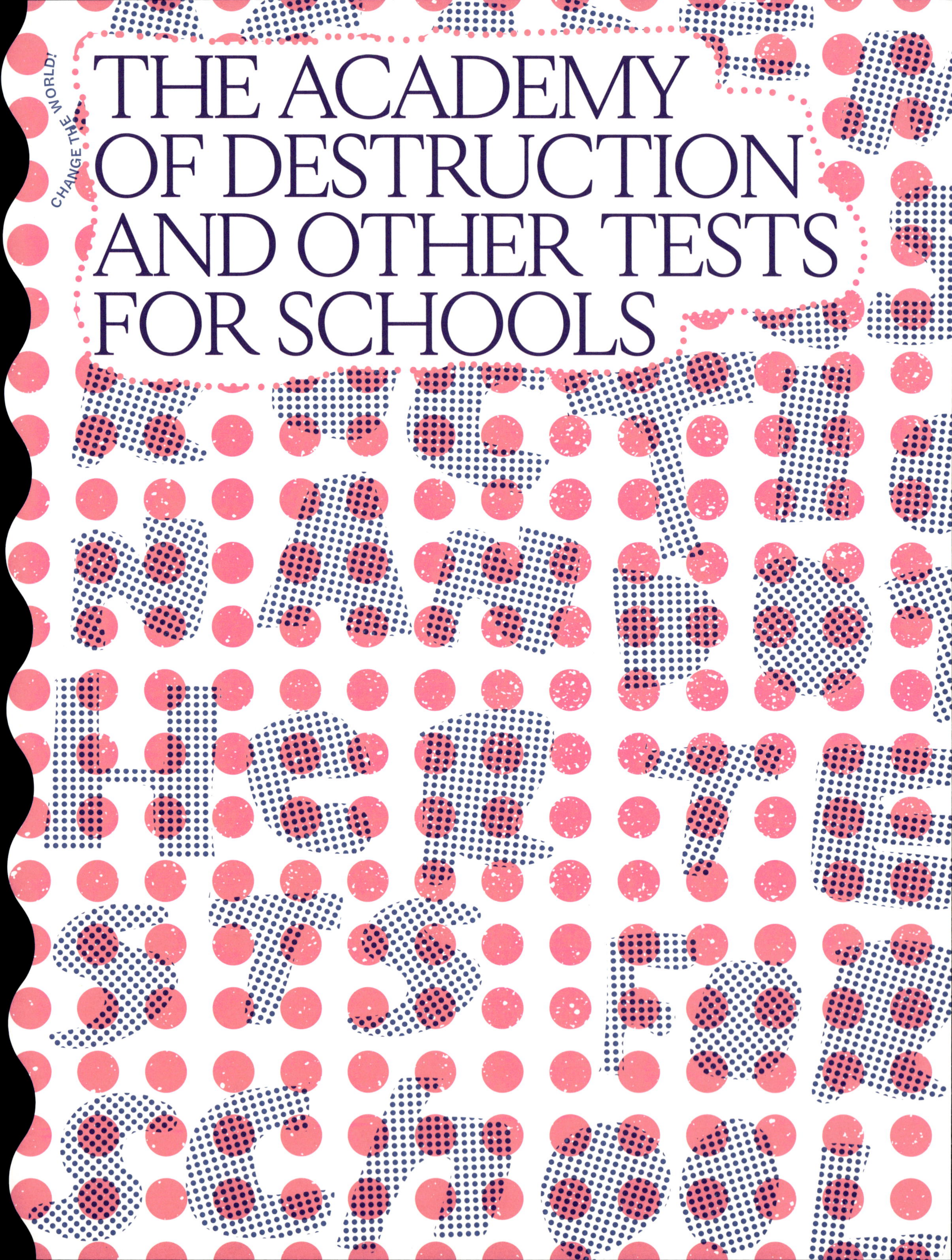
CHANGE THE WORLD!
THE ACADEMY OF DESTRUCTION AND OTHER TESTS FOR SCHOOLS

Because Theatre of Research conducts research together with children, we often visit schools, because that's where children spend most of their days. We have therefore also questioned power plays in schools. What about the one between students and teachers? Children are usually tested and graded in schools by the adults. This can cause a lot of damage, too, as you surely know. Grades and tests are stressful and often not fair. What if the kids tested their schools instead for once? What could a test like that look like?

Outside of school, when children are playing, all sorts of objects can play along. For example, you might be a princess and bang a large vase with a spoon to make it sound like the gong in the throne hall. As you know, that's one of the ways children do their own kind of research while playing. At school, on the other hand, we often find that objects are only allowed to be used for

one

thing. The banisters must never be used as slides, and the chairs must never be used as seesaws, and so on. This often causes problems because children keep trying to use things for something other than what they were made for. And then they get in trouble for it. That's not fair. Therefore, in the school crash test, we turn things around, and it goes like this:

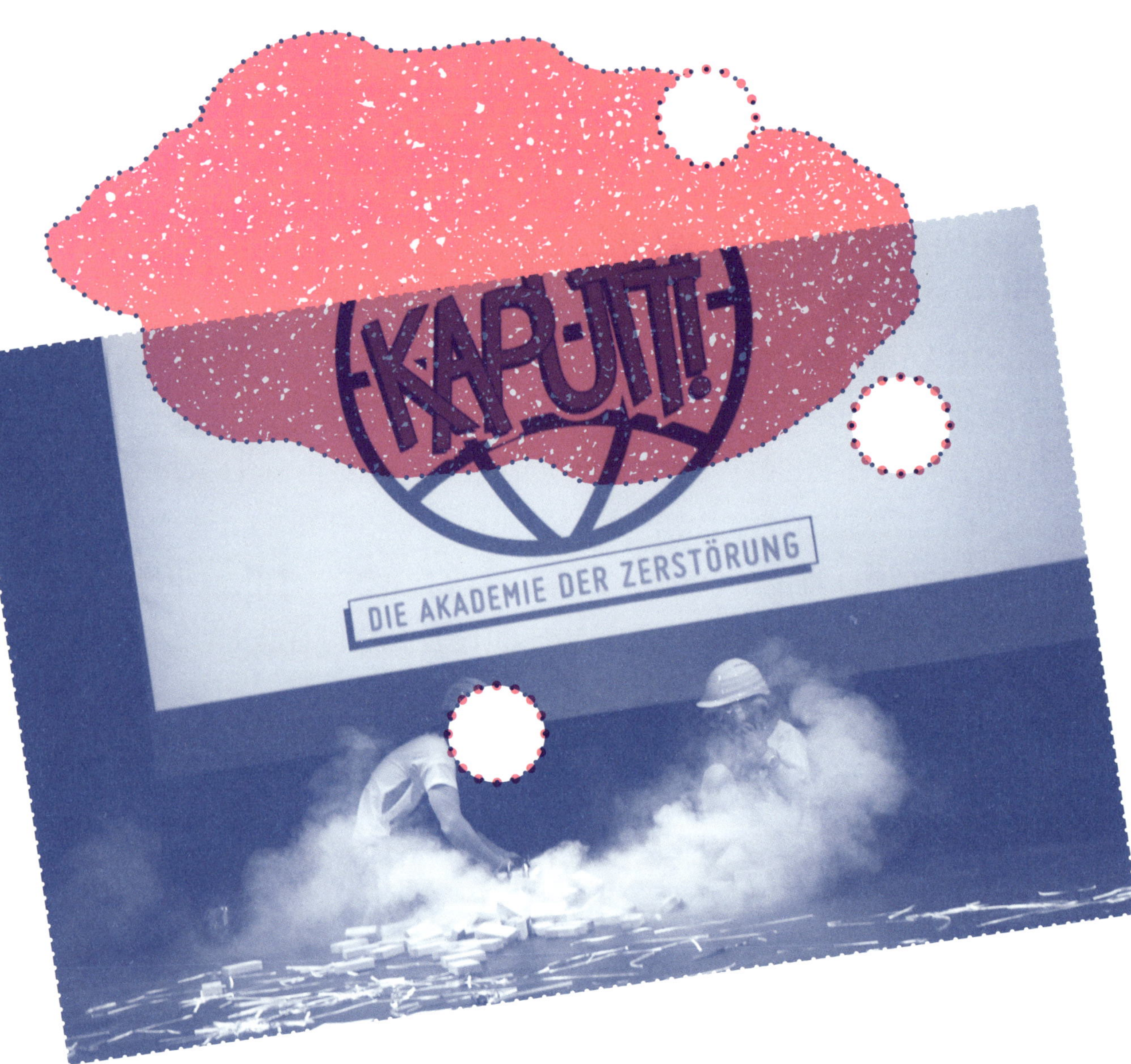
KAPUTT!
DIE AKADEMIE DER ZERSTÖRUNG

SCHOOL CRASH TEST[12]

1. Ten children are appointed crash testers. Each of them selects one thing to be used differently, as something else. For example: Can a school desk serve as a drum kit? Can the large pillows from the relaxation room become a sled to slide down the stairs? Is the table tennis table suitable as a trampoline?

2. After ten such ideas are collected, the children go and ask:

May we borrow the pillows? We'll put a plastic bag around them, so they don't get dirty?

Can we just be really loud really loud for a moment — for about 15 minutes?

Can we get on the ping-pong table and try something out?

12 School Crash Test was developed and conducted with Florian Feigl and Jens-Jakob de Place as part of the Children Testing Schools Programme in 2008. About a dozen schools participated in the program.

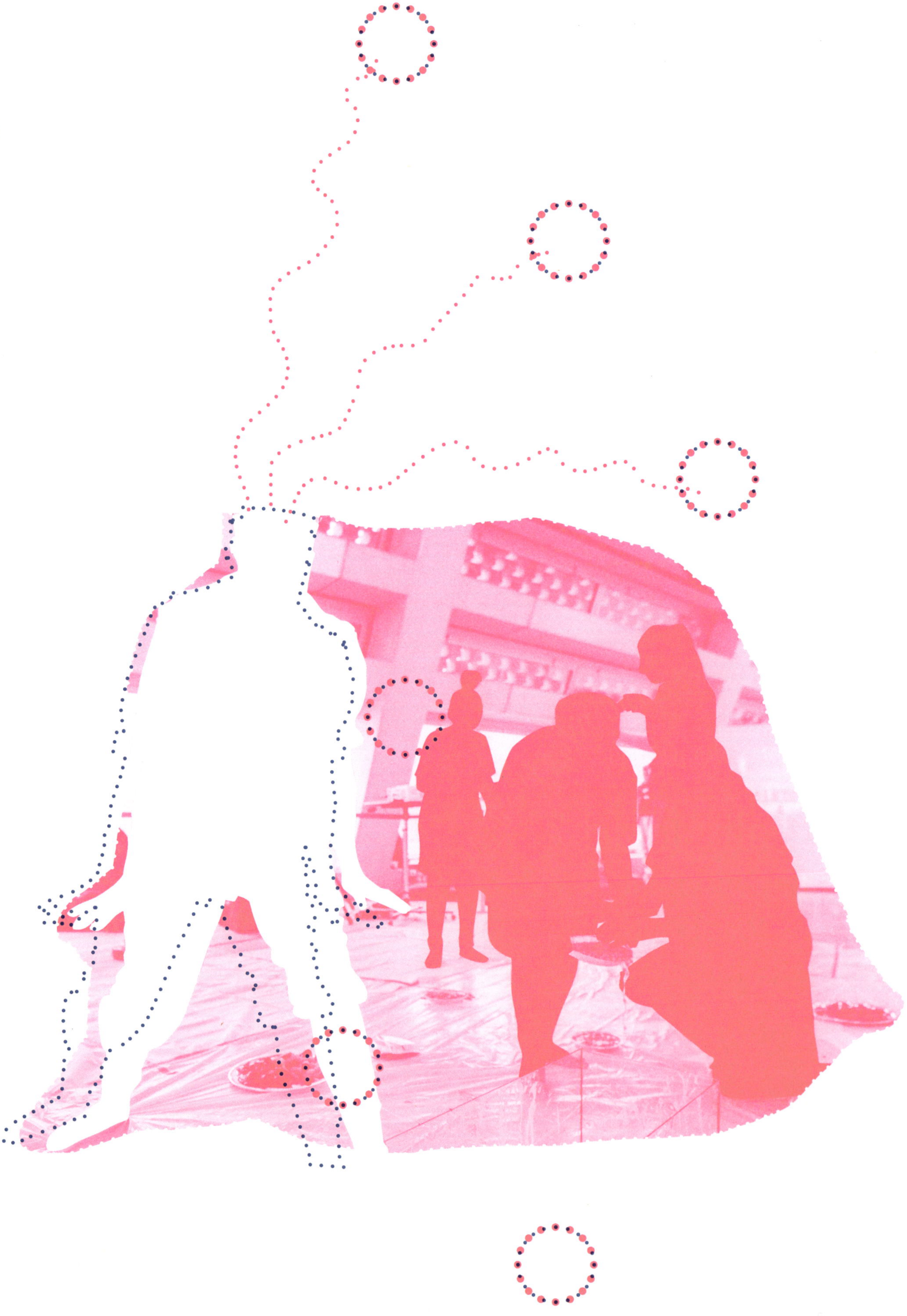

3. And that is exactly the test: The school can get ten out of ten points if all ten ideas can be tried out. Points are deducted for every one that's *not allowed*. There are additional points for special commitment. A certificate is then written for the school administration. For example, eight out of ten points is pretty good. If more than one school is tested, you can compare!

Would you like to conduct a crash test?
What should be turned into what?

Often the ideas the kids wanted to try were a bit dangerous, like: Could all the chairs in the auditorium be built into a five-meter high tower? Adults are then afraid that something bad could happen. And they are also afraid that this will not be covered by insurance. Every time an accident happens in schools or daycares, this is reported to the insurance companies. The insurance companies evaluate it and

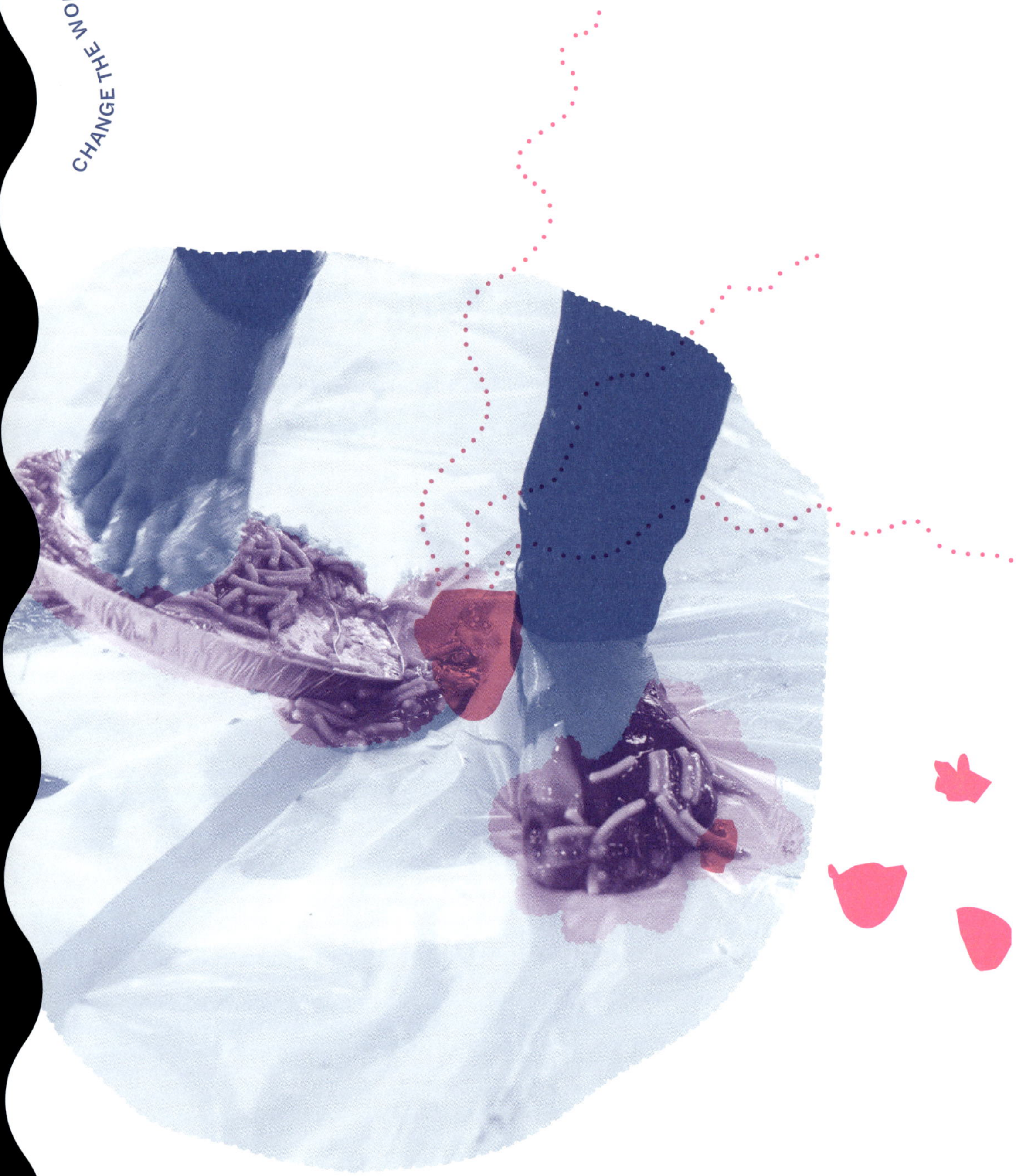

then write a letter to everyone stating what new precautionary measures should be taken. That's good, because then fewer accidents happen. At the same time, it is also bad because there are more and more precautionary rules. And then there are fewer and fewer options for children to transform and create. And then the world becomes just what it is, instead of what it could be. In Theatre of Research we turned this into an interactive play called *Danger! Danger! 50 Dangerous Things You Should Let Your Children Do.*[13] In this play we invite the kids from the audience to try out how fire extinguishers work, to make inflatables explode, to light matches, to glue their fingertips together and lick batteries. Together we confront our most dangerous ideas — but with care. When was the last time you did something dangerous?

If you want to try something dangerous, you have to team up and prepare together: You should talk about what could happen and then take precautions, for example, with safety goggles or padding or by roping up. A danger zone may also need to be marked out and a signal may be used to warn at the beginning and end of the action. That can be great fun.

However, some of the children who took part in the school crash tests wanted to break something above all else. They didn't want to build the chairs into a tower, they wanted to throw them straight out of the window. They probably had their reasons for that. That got

13 *Danger! Danger! 50 Dangerous Things You Should Let Your Children Do* by Sibylle Peters and Hanno Krieg was first presented in 2013. *50 Dangerous Things (You Should Let Your Children Do)* is also the title of a fantastic book, full of instructions, by Tinkering Unlimited.

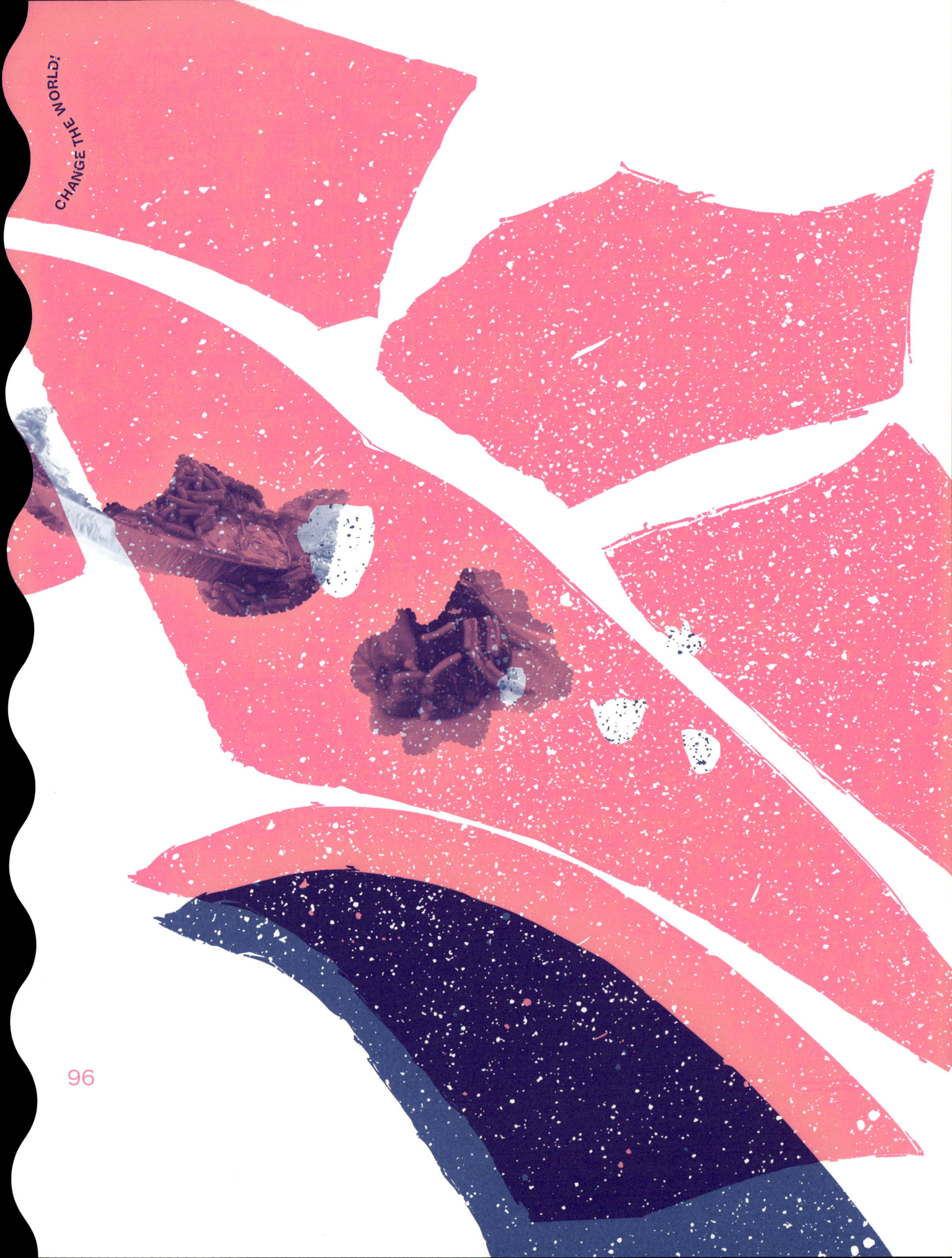

us thinking. There are many children who wish to break something. Usually, the result is that they are no longer allowed to participate. Because you can't break something on purpose, can you?

In live art you can. The artist Yoko Ono, for example, had the spectators of her performance cut the dress she was wearing to pieces. Artist Stephen Cripps built a helicopter rotor in such a way that with each rotation it scratched the wall of the room a tiny bit more. And the artist Gustav Metzger even founded an entire art movement based on destruction. As a child in Germany, he had to flee from the Nazis. Metzger felt that we should experiment with destruction in art rather than in reality. And he's certainly right about that.

That's why Theatre of Research founded the Academy of Destruction.[14] Six children who liked to break stuff and six artists who were familiar with the art of destruction were the professors of this academy. Each professor—meaning the adult artists and the children—prepared a lesson for the academy in which something was to be broken. A child and an adult then gave their lesson together. For example, twelve-year-old Kevin and the artist Armin Chodzinski gave the following lesson: Kevin smashed a school desk with a karate kick and talked about why he felt like destroying everything at school. Armin then talked about guitar destruction in the history of art and music. Afterwards, Armin and Kevin and the audience gave a guitar destruction concert together. Of course, everyone had to wear gloves and safety goggles.

14 The Academy of Destruction was founded together with the Live Art Development Agency and Tate Learning / Tate Exchange London in 2017.

At the Academy of Destruction, we have explored many exciting questions, such as: Is destruction always a bad thing? Who decides what counts as destruction and what is called something else? Whenever something is produced or designed, for example a car, something else is destroyed to make it. Most of the time we just don't pay attention to that. Who decides when it's worth it to destroy something and build something else, and when it isn't?

What do you think about that?

Would you like to destroy something, too? What?

Draw it or write it down on this page, then tear the page out of the book and crumple it up as much as you can.

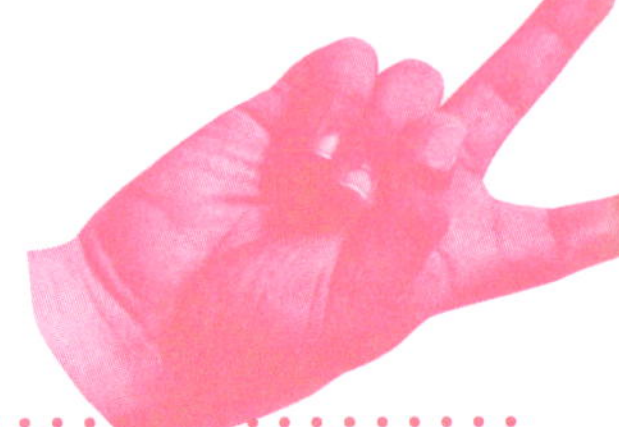

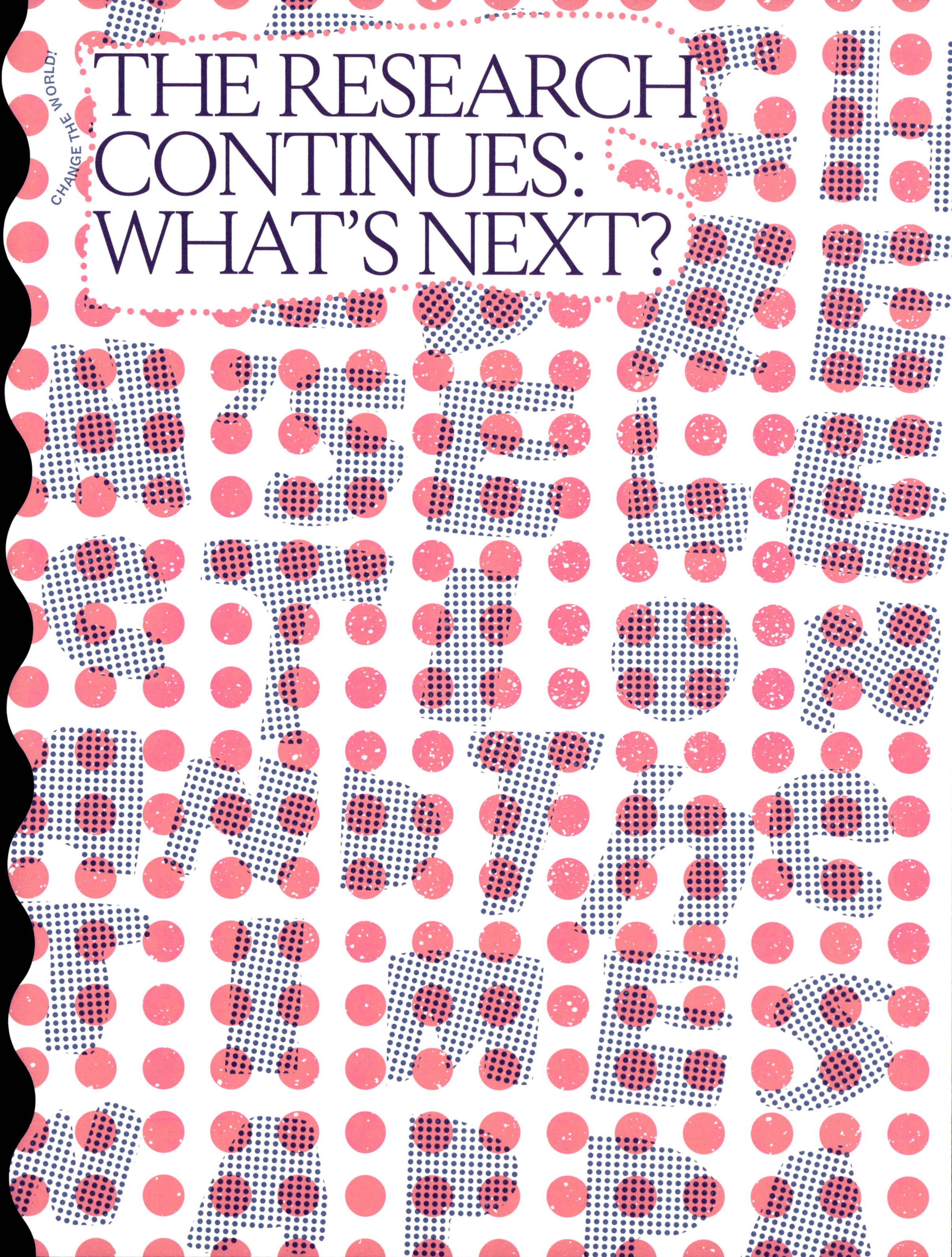
CHANGE THE WORLD!
THE RESEARCH CONTINUES: WHAT'S NEXT?

In this book we told you about some of the most beautiful research stories that we have experienced since Theatre of Research was founded twenty years ago. But there are many more. It is difficult to decide which ones might be most interesting for you. For example, we went looking for miracles and asked different people if they had ever experienced a miracle.[15] Most had some pretty great stories to tell. We would like to tell you about these miracles, but unfortunately, we are running out of time, because our research continues and we need to get back to our current experiments.

Right now, we are researching the wish to be beautiful. We all want to be beautiful, don't we?

This research was a suggestion by our theater consultants. This is a group of children who experience racism in their daily lives. They propose new ideas to our theater once a year. One of those is the Alternative Beauty Salon, which we are working on right now. We have spoken to many children and adults and they often do not feel so beautiful. For example, they feel too fat, too pimply, too old, too dark, and so on. They said that by the fourth grade, the trouble with beauty already starts—and then it never really stops. Why is that?

For certain, racism, sexism, and ageism and their deeply unfair prejudgments about people have something to do with it. In addition, a lot of money is made from beauty products. But if we all felt beautiful already, we couldn't be sold beauty products anymore. Therefore, the beauty industry is making us feel bad about ourselves on

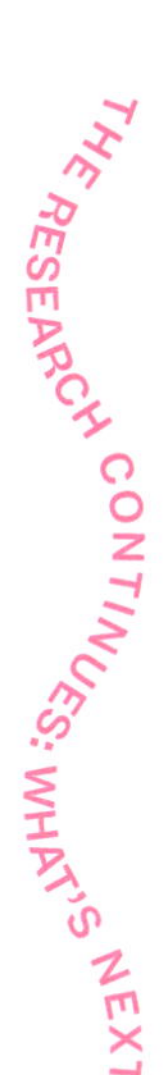

15 The Search for Miracles was conducted together with Matthias Anton, Sylvia Deinert, Tine Krieg, and Tanja Gwiasda first in 2009.

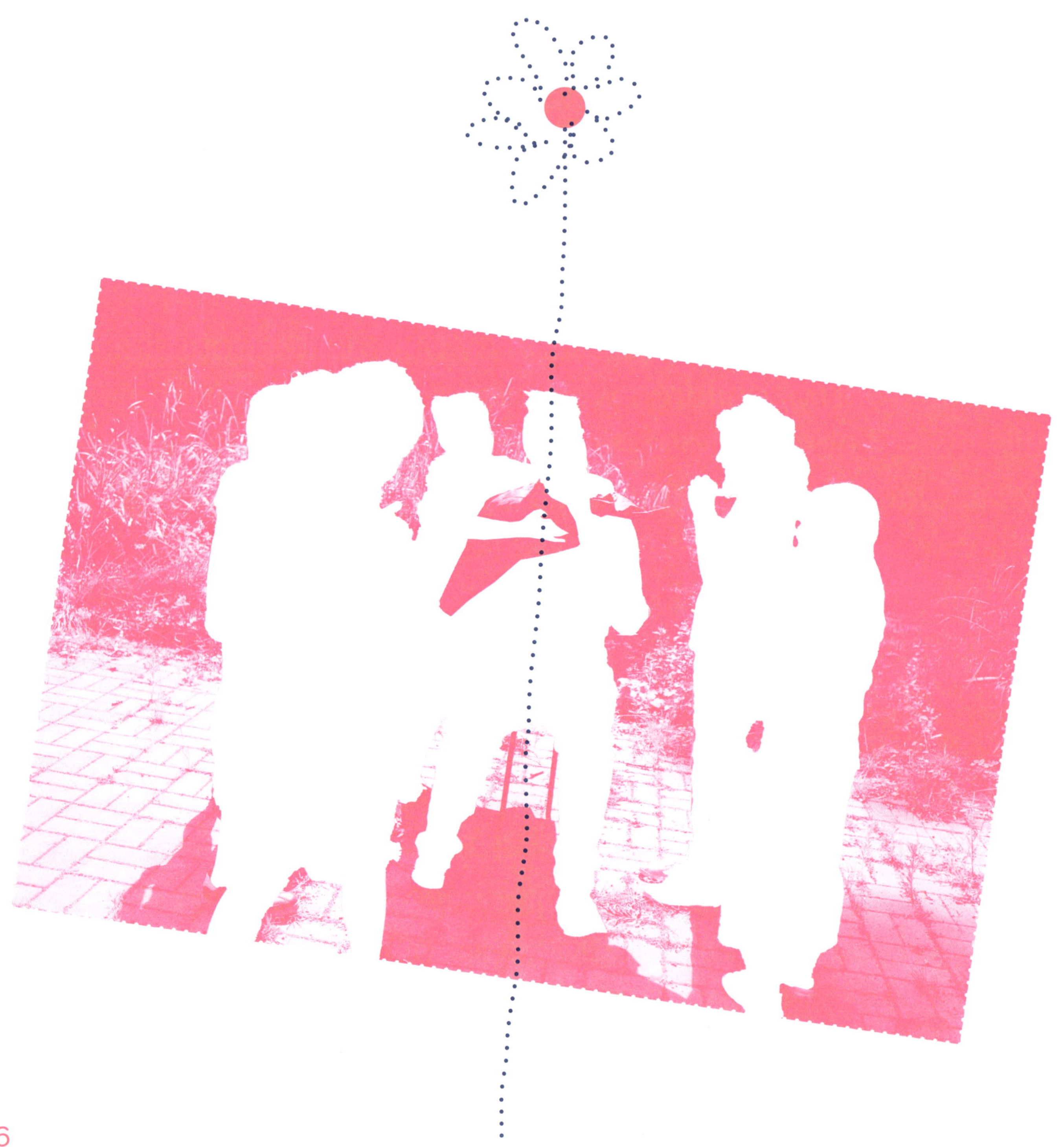

purpose. What can we at Theatre of Research do to make us all feel more beautiful?

That's what we want to find out in the Alternative Beauty Salon. We try to push our feeling-beautiful-meter upwards: How can we succeed in feeling more beautiful together? Or do we prefer to enjoy being really ugly for once? Come by the beauty salon and do some research with us![16]

Of course, it is possible that you will not read these lines until much later, when the Alternative Beauty Salon is already over. But by then there will be another type of research that you can take part in. What do you think,

what
should
we
explore
next?

Send us
a
research
assignment!

16
The Alternative Beauty Salon, which opened in 2023, is a collaboration with Brenda Alais, Alexandra Owusu, Sarife Afonso, and others. The Salon invites kids and adults from the age of nine to participate.

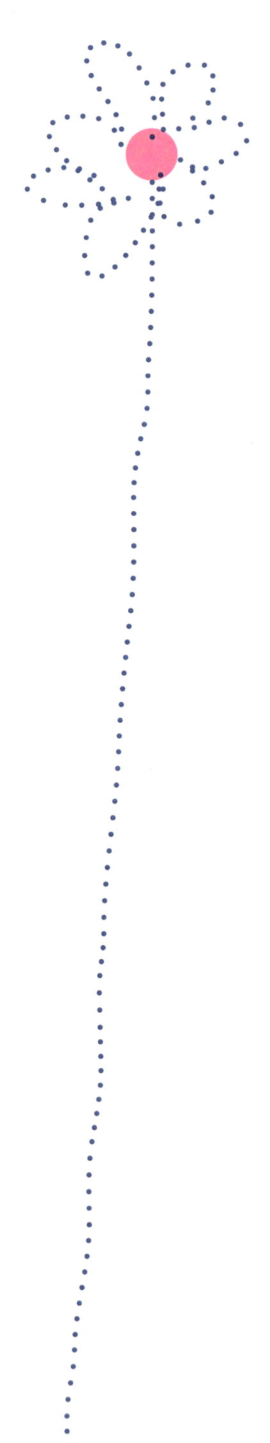

From:

To: FUNDUS THEATER / Forschungstheater
Sievekingdamm 3,
Square of Children's Rights
20535 Hamburg, Germany

fold here

My idea:

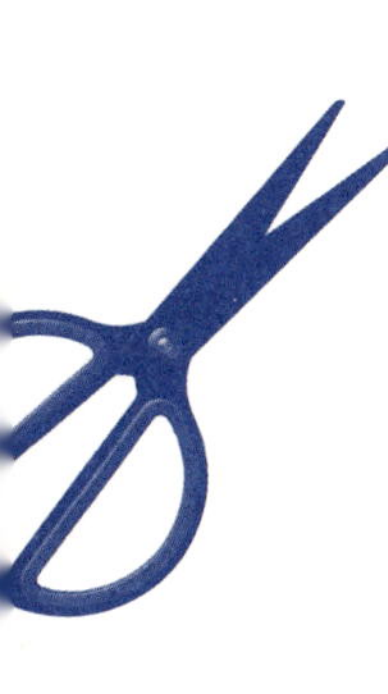

CHANGE THE WORLD!

Sibylle Peters is an artist and researcher based in Hamburg, Germany. She founded Theatre of Research in 2003. She lives with her son Jim, her friends, and her cat in St. Pauli, Hamburg. To learn about other parts of her work, for example in feminist seafaring or the theatre of touch, go to wishfulthinking.eu.

Author's Note

This book was first written in German and published for the 20th anniversary of Theatre of Research in 2023. I then translated the book into English with the invaluable support of Lois Keidan. The English manuscript was then edited by Thick Press. Thanks to Omnivore for their vision of a hybrid between fairytale and workbook, and thanks to Erin Segal and Rachel Kauder Nalebuff for their careful reading and feedback. Thanks to all members of FUNDUS THEATER/ Forschungstheater in Hamburg and to all the kids, who changed the world with us.
—SP

SOURCE MATERIALS USED IN ILLUSTRATIONS AND COLLAGES COURTESY OF:

p.12 Margaux Weiß
p.14 Michael Coester
p.16 Theatre of Research
p.20 Heinrich Mandt
p.22 Hanno Krieg
p.24 Hanno Krieg
p.26 Hanno Krieg
p.34 Michael Coester
p.36 Matthias Anton
p.38 Heinrich Mandt
p.44 participant, unkown
p.46 Ellen Coenders
p.48 Ellen Coenders
p.50 Ellen Coenders
p.54 Ellen Coenders
p.56 Ellen Coenders
p.62 Margaux Weiß
p.64 Theatre of Research
p.66 Heinrich Mandt (showing Angela Bartram in her piece “Human School”)
p.68 Angela von Brill
p.70 Heinrich Mandt
p.82 Margaux Weiß
p.84 Margaux Weiß
p.90 Katharina Duve
p.92 Tate Photography
p.94 Tate Photography
p.96 Tate Photography
p.106 Margaux Weiß

THE RESEARCH CONTINUES: WHAT'S NEXT?

Published by Thick Press thickpress.com

ISBN: 978-1-7320666-5-6

Book design, illustrations, and collages by Omnivore, Inc.

Editing: Thick Press

Typefaces: HB Hue designed by Hyo Kwon and Berton Hasebe

Halyard designed by Joshua Darden along with Eben Sorkin and Lucas Sharp

Kessler Italic by Production Type

Union designed by Radim Peško

Printing: Asia Pacific Offset

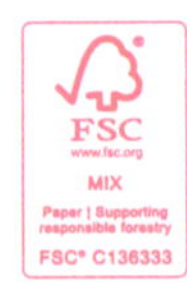